THE POWER
o f PRAYER
AND FASTING

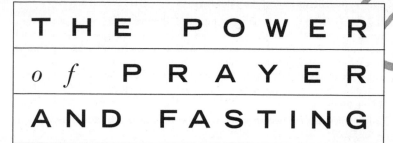

THE POWER
o f PRAYER
AND FASTING

MARILYN HICKEY

FaithWords

New York   Boston   Nashville

The health advice in this book is not intended to replace the services of a trained health professional. Fasting can be dangerous and you are advised to consult with your health care professional with regard to all matters relating to your health, and in particular regarding matters which may require diagnosis or medical attention. If you are pregnant, overweight or have other special conditions requiring attention, you should seek a professional opinion and consider modification of the fasting program.

Unless otherwise specified, all Scripture references are from the King James Version of the Bible.

Scriptures noted CEV are taken from THE CONTEMPORARY VERSION. Copyright © 1991 by the American Bible Society. Used by permission.

Scriptures noted NIV are taken from the HOLY BIBLE: NEW INTERNATIONAL VERSION®. Copyright © 1973, 1978, 1984 by International Bible Society. Used by permission of Zondervan Publishing House.

Scriptures noted NKJV are taken from the New King James Version. Copyright © 1979, 1980, 1982 by Thomas Nelson, Inc. Used by permission.

FaithWords
Hachette Book Group USA
237 Park Avenue
New York, NY 10169
Visit our Web site at www.faithwords.com

Printed in the United States of America

First Warner Faith Edition: February 2006

10 9 8 7 6 5 4

The FaithWords name and logo are trademarks of Hachette Book Group USA.

Library of Congress Cataloging-in-Publication Data

Hickey, Marilyn.
    The power of prayer and fasting : 21 days that can change your life / Marilyn Hickey.— 1st ed.
       p. cm.
    Summary: "Television host Marilyn Hickey reveals the power and benefits of the discipline of fasting in her 21-day program."—provided by the publisher.
    ISBN 978-0-446-69498-8
  1. Spiritual life—Christianity. 2. Prayer—Christianity. 3. Fasting—Religious aspects—Christianity. I. Title.
    BV4501.3.H52 2006
    248.4'7—dc22   2005022813

To my son-in-law, Reece Bowling, and my daughter, Sarah Bowling. Reece is better than a son; he is like seven sons to me. He is prayerful, encouraging, and sympathetic. Sarah has always been a good friend to me, but now she is my best spiritual friend. Sometimes I wonder how I can be so blessed!

CONTENTS

ACKNOWLEDGMENTS

I want to express my gratitude and acknowledge the contribution of Dr. Augustine Obinnah to this book. Dr. Obinnah is a physician I have come to know and respect; he and his family are members of our church congregation at Orchard Road Christian Center in Denver.

I asked Dr. Obinnah to do a thorough review of this manuscript prior to publication, and offer his medical insights on the subject of fasting, which have been incorporated into the text.

Thanks as well to Bob Rodgers for permitting me to use his comprehensive fasting program materials.

I also appreciate the online resource by Dr. Elson M. Haas, "Nutritional Program for Fasting," and the online resource from Freedomyou.com titled "How to Break a Fast."

WHY I PERSONALLY FAST AND PRAY

I not only teach people to fast and pray. I personally fast and pray. I have done so for the past forty-five years.

Why?

First, I have found that prayer and fasting go together like conjoined twins that cannot be divided. When I am in prolonged and fervent prayer, I automatically find that I have less desire for food—indeed, less need for food. When I feel a need to cleanse my physical system through modified forms of fasting, I nearly always find that I have a greater longing to cleanse all aspects of my life—especially my spirit—through longer and more intense times of prayer with the Lord.

Second, as I have observed many ministers who are truly anointed of God and are highly effective in both reaching the lost and taking God's healing power to people in great need, I have concluded that fasting and prayer are integral parts of their lives. An emphasis on prayer, accompanied by fasting, appears to be a very serious component of any ministry that results in life-changing conversions and miracles.

Third, I have found in my personal life that when I fast as part of a time of focused and intense prayer, I am more sensitive to the

Holy Spirit, the voice of God, and I am better able to discern the direction God desires for me to take. Fasting helps me to "put down" my flesh and opens me to the still, small voice of the Lord. I usually find that after a fast, I have renewed enthusiasm and even greater courage for undertaking the tasks the Lord has set before me.

I have not engaged in what I consider to be prolonged fasting. My husband has been led by God to go on several forty-day fasts in his life. He has also experienced twenty-one-day and ten-day fasts.

Prolonged fasting of this type is hard on my body. The Lord gave me a personal pattern for fasting when I first began to teach. He led me to fast and pray seven meals a week. I found that I could do these in any order—for example, I could fast one meal and eat two meals a day for each of seven days, or I might eat two meals a day for three days, eat only one meal a day for two days, and eat three meals for two days. For years, I followed a pattern of fasting seven meals a week except when I was on vacation with my family. This practice helped me greatly in staying at a consistent place in my spiritual life so I could hear God's voice plainly.

If you study the early church, you will find that a number of the church fathers wrote about fasting and practiced those disciplines often. The Roman Catholic Church has recommended fasting for hundreds of years. The Protestant denominations, however, have not placed an emphasis on fasting, largely, I believe, because Protestant leaders in the last hundred years have not done a great deal of teaching about fasting and praying or encouraged people to do it.

Years ago I had an opportunity to travel to South Korea and to visit with Dr. Paul Yonggi Cho's mother-in-law, who was the leader at a retreat center called Prayer Mountain outside Seoul. She, along with Dr. Cho, believed that prayer and fasting are what birthed a great revival in South Korea so that today, the nation is 40 percent Christian, when it formerly was 98 percent Buddhist. In attending services and board meetings with Dr. Cho, I learned a great deal about combining fasting and prayer, and especially fasting and praying in the Spirit. Much of what I know today about fasting and prayer I learned from Dr. Cho and his mother-in-law.

I also learned valuable lessons about fasting and prayer from my mother. When my father was admitted to a mental hospital and the attending psychiatrists told my mother that he would never come out of that hospital, my mother immediately began to fast and pray for his healing. Within a year, my father was born again, baptized in water, and out of that hospital! I believe my father is in heaven today largely because of my mother's practice of fasting and praying for him during the months of his illness.

I thank God for the way that fasting and prayer open the heavens so we might experience an outpouring of God's power and blessings. I am 100 percent convinced that these practices are musts for believers.

A LONG-STANDING COMMITMENT TO FASTING AND PRAYING

About fifteen years ago, we began a more formal program of fasting and praying in our church in Colorado. We called it "21 Days of Prayer and Fasting." We have done this at the beginning of each year, and we have found that our church comes out of this three-week time of prayer and fasting highly energized, highly focused, and highly unified to undertake the ministry challenges God has revealed to us as a body.

During the three weeks of prayer and fasting, we have special prayer meetings—including added prayer meetings early in the morning, at noontime, and some evenings. These additional meetings give all members of the pastoral staff an opportunity to lead in prayer, which is important both to them and to the people in our church. We also have designated nights for people to pray and then to write down their personal, spiritual, family, material, and financial goals for the coming year. We have special times of prayer for specific needs. Our entire ministry staff and church staff participate, as do the majority of the members of our congregation.

Through the years, my husband has led a Monday night prayer meeting. During these first three weeks of the year, that prayer meeting becomes part of the "21 Days of Prayer and Fasting."

The results have been absolutely wonderful. There's a fresh anointing in our church services and at times, unusual answers to prayer. It seems to me that our altar calls—when we call people to come forward and receive Jesus Christ as their Savior—are more intense and fruitful. We also see ongoing answers to prayer throughout the year. It is not at all unusual for someone to say months later, "God has answered a prayer I prayed during the '21 Days of Prayer and Fasting'!"

The "21 Days of Prayer and Fasting" produces very real and strong bonds among the people who undertake this program together. Their hearts are knit together in unusual ways. Many people have reported that in the weeks that follow this program, they find they need to do less "remedial" prayer to fix problems or resolve a crisis that may arise. Rather, they find themselves engaging in preventive prayer to put a stop to the enemy before he has a chance to gain even a toehold in their lives.

There's an entire chapter on this twenty-one-day fast later in this book.

CONSISTENCY AND STRENGTH

Finally, and this is of the utmost importance, an ongoing pattern of prayer and fasting has given me a consistency in my spiritual life. It has given me a consistency in receiving insights into God's Word. Plain and simple, I get more out of my Bible reading when I accompany it with regular prayer and fasting.

I also experience greater consistency in overcoming the attacks of the enemy against my life. I believe very strongly that I have not fallen into many of the pits that the devil had prepared for me because I was praying and fasting regularly and had the ability to discern various pitfalls in advance.

All persons have areas of weakness in their lives, and I believe strongly that prayer and fasting give people strength in areas of weakness. Sometimes it is strength that prepares a person in advance to deal with problems that might arise. Sometimes it is strength to compensate for personal weaknesses. Sometimes it is strength to overcome mistakes.

Certainly a practice of prayer and fasting does not keep a person from failing, stumbling, or doing dumb things from time to time. In more than forty years of pastoring a church with my husband, and in more than thirty years of leading a television and radio ministry, I have done some dumb things. But God, in His great mercy, brought me through those mistakes and gave me the insight and courage to overcome and reverse the mistakes, and in the end, emerge stronger and more effective for the gospel. I believe prayer and fasting paved the way for me to make it through very difficult times—it gave me the spiritual strength necessary to overcome and to persevere.

There's a saying that goes something like this: "If you always do the same thing, don't be surprised when you get the same results." Most people feel compelled to begin a time of prayer and fasting because they don't like the results they have been getting from prayer alone. There is a need in their lives. They sense that they need to do something more, something differently, or something new to have a breakthrough or to reach a new level of spiritual maturity.

For many people, that something new is prayer coupled with fasting. I strongly recommend this biblical practice to you.

—*Marilyn Hickey*

PART I

GOD'S CALL TO PRAY AND FAST

1

FASTING AND PRAYER ARE FOR THE CHURCH TODAY

"Fasting and prayer? Didn't those go out of style decades ago?" The woman who said this to me was a godly woman, a woman who had been in the church all her life, and a woman intent on obeying the Lord. She knew her Bible. She was very serious in her questions.

Yet for some reason, she had concluded—at least subconsciously—that fasting and prayer were no longer intended for believers in today's world.

The truth is, fasting and prayer are for today! In fact, now more than ever!

The combination of fasting and praying is not a fad or a novelty approach to spiritual discipline. Fasting and praying are not part of a human-engineered method or plan. They are not the means to manipulate a situation or to create a circumstance. Fasting and praying are Bible-based disciplines that are appropriate for all believers of all ages throughout all centuries in all parts of the world.

Through the years, I have learned that many people in the church have never been taught about fasting and prayer, and many have therefore never fasted and prayed. As a result, they don't know why fasting and praying are important, what the Bible teaches about fasting, or how to fast. To many, fasting sounds like drudgery—or a form of religious works. To others, fasting sounds extremely difficult. People tend to stand in awe at reports of those who have fasted for several weeks. When I hear about such fasts, I no doubt think what they think: *If I fasted that long, I'd die! I couldn't possibly do that!*

Let me assure you at the outset of this book that I am not advocating prolonged periods of fasting for every believer. A fast can be as short as one meal. Neither do I advocate fasting and praying for the mere sake of saying with self-righteousness, "I have fasted and prayed about this." I do not advocate fasting so that the hungry in a foreign nation might have the food you would have eaten that day—which is highly unlikely. I do not advocate fasting apart from *prayer.*

KEY REASONS TO FAST AND PRAY

I do, however, encourage every believer to fast and pray for two very important reasons:

1. The Scriptures Teach Us to Fast and Pray

The Bible has a great deal to say about both fasting and praying, including commands to fast and pray. The Bible also gives us examples of people who fasted and prayed, using different types of fasts for different reasons, all of which are very positive results. Jesus fasted and prayed. Jesus' disciples fasted and prayed after the Resurrection. Many of the Old Testament heroes and heroines of the faith fasted and prayed. The followers of John the Baptist fasted and prayed. Many people in the early church fasted and prayed. What the Scriptures have taught us directly and by the examples of the saints is surely something we are to do.

2. Fasting and Prayer Put You into the Best Possible Position for a Breakthrough

That breakthrough might be in the realm of the spirit. It may be in the realm of your emotions or personal habits. It may be in the realm of a very practical area of life, such as a relationship or finances. What I have seen repeatedly through the years—not only in the Scriptures but in countless personal stories that others have told me—is that periods of fasting and prayer produce great spiritual results, many of which fall into the realm of a breakthrough. What wasn't a reality . . . suddenly was. What hadn't worked . . . suddenly did. The unwanted situation or object that was there . . . suddenly wasn't there. The relationship that was unloving . . . suddenly was loving. The job that hadn't materialized . . . suddenly did.

The very simple and direct conclusions I draw are these: First, if the Bible teaches us to do something, I want to do it. I want to obey the Lord in every way that He commands me to obey Him. And second, if fasting and praying are means to a breakthrough that God has for me, I want to undertake those disciplines so I might experience that breakthrough!

Every person I know needs a breakthrough in some area of his or her life. I am no exception. I need breakthroughs all the time—it may be a breakthrough in understanding a situation, a breakthrough answer to a problem, a breakthrough idea, a breakthrough insight, a breakthrough in financial or material provision, a breakthrough in health. If you have any need in your life, you need a breakthrough from God to meet that need! Fasting and prayer break the yoke of bondage and bring about a release of God's presence, power, and provision.

I certainly have seen this borne out in the course of my ministry.

When I was forty-two years old, I went to an Assemblies of God camp in Alexandria, Minnesota, to speak for a women's retreat. The first two days of the retreat went very well, and then I had one day in between the first retreat and the second—so many women had registered, the camp could not host all of the women at the same time. I took that day in this lovely place in Minnesota to enjoy the lakes and trees—it was a gorgeous environment—and to fast and pray about God's will for my life. I felt as if I was doing a lot of good things, but I also thought I might miss God's best for me. I longed to hear from God and to receive a revelation from Him about my life.

In that day of fasting and prayer, God spoke to me words from Isaiah 11:9: "I have called you to cover the earth with the Word." Through the years, the Lord has confirmed that word to me a number of times, but this was my initial call to take the message of God's Word to the whole earth, and it came as the result of one day of prayer and fasting.

The breakthrough that you may need in your life is a sense of God's direction—not only for today and tomorrow, but for the broad scope of your life. If you long to know God's purpose for you on this earth, I strongly encourage you to seek God in prayer and fasting.

THE PRINCIPLES OF BIBLICAL FASTING

There are two main overriding principles related to prayer and fasting in the Bible.

First, biblical fasting is going without food. The noun translated "fast" or "a fasting" is *tsom* in the Hebrew and *nesteia* in the Greek language. It means the voluntary abstinence from food. The literal Hebrew translation would be "not to eat." The literal Greek means "no food."

I know people who say they go without television or movies, and they call these "fasting" times. I'm not opposed to that definition of fasting—fasting does imply that we are giving up one thing in order to replace it with something else, and in the Bible sense, specifically to replace it with prayer. But in the main, I believe fasting has to do with our abstaining from *food*.

Second, biblical fasting is linked with serious seasons of prayer. The more seriously we approach prayer *and* fasting, the more serious the results we will experience.

I sometimes hear people say, "I'm giving up chocolate" and they regard this as a type of fasting. I think this is a rather frivolous approach. The first and foremost purpose of a biblical or spiritual fast is to get a breakthrough on a particular matter that one lifts up to the Lord in prayer. A spiritual fast involves our hearts and the way in which we relate to and trust God. It relates to discerning and receiving strength to follow through on what God might reveal to us about circumstances in our lives or a direction we are to take.

I am not against people fasting in order to lose weight. Many people fast to lose weight or maintain their weight. What I am opposed to is making the losing of weight your primary goal in a season of spiritual fasting and prayer. To have weight loss as a goal makes your fasting a diet plan, not a time of genuine fasting and prayer. If losing weight is your purpose in fasting, you will be missing out on the full reason for fasting, and you likely will be concerned only with what you *don't eat* rather than with what you *are led to pray.*

Now there's certainly an issue of food that is associated with many seasons of prayer and fasting, and let me quickly add this: control of eating is a valid reason to fast. The purpose is not the number of pounds you might lose during a fast, but rather, trusting God to help you regain mastery over food during a fast. Jesus said, "The spirit is . . . willing, but the flesh is weak" (Matt. 26:41). Fasting is a means of bringing the flesh into submission to the Lord so He can strengthen us in our mastery over our own selves. Fasting in the flesh makes us stronger to stand against the temptations of the flesh. Those temptations very often deal with food.

Abstaining from food is often God's way of showing that His desire for us is that we regain mastery over all things associated with our flesh in order to subdue our flesh and elevate our emphasis on spiritual matters. God's promise is to help us as we overcome the flesh and put all carnal temptations into subjection.

ABSTAINING FROM FOOD
TO REGAIN MASTERY OF THE FLESH

We are wise to recognize that food was the enticement the devil used to cause Eve and Adam to sin in the Garden of Eden. In Genesis 2 the Lord God told Adam and Eve that they could eat freely of every tree in the garden of Eden, "but of the tree of the knowledge of good and evil, thou shalt not eat of it: for in the day that thou eatest thereof thou shalt surely die" (Gen. 2:17). God did not tell Adam and Eve to refrain from touching a particular animal or smelling a particular flower or swimming in a certain stream. He told them to refrain from taking a particular fruit into their bodies—one type of fruit out of all the many types He had made available to them.

God had given Adam and Eve authority over all things that He had created—every bird, fish, beast of the field, and over "every herb bearing seed, which is upon the face of all the earth, and every tree, in which is the fruit of a tree yielding seed; to you it shall be for meat" (Gen. 1:29). God did not prohibit Adam and Eve from interacting with any part of God's creation when He commanded them to be fruitful, multiply, replenish the earth, and subdue it—except for this one tree and its fruit. They were not to eat of a particular tree, what God described to them as the "tree of the knowledge of good and evil."

Why did God set apart this one tree and its fruit? God was giving Adam and Eve free will and the ability to make choices and decisions. Free will isn't really free if a person has no *choice*.

Adam and Eve had a choice to make about this one tree. God told them to abstain from eating from its fruit because He did not want His beloved creation to have a knowledge of evil. He had already given them a full knowledge of everything He called "good." He wanted to spare them the heartache of knowing evil.

That's true for us today as Christians. God calls us to pursue only what is good. Paul wrote to the Philippians: "Whatsoever things are true . . . honest . . . just . . . pure . . . lovely . . . of good report; if there be any virtue, and if there be any praise, think on these things" (Phil. 4:8). God desires only good for His children. He tells us in His Word, "Be not overcome of evil, but overcome evil with good" (Rom. 12:21).

Even as God calls us away from evil and toward good, He gives us a choice. So many of the problems we have in our world today are the result of men and women making the wrong choices. They have knowingly and unknowingly chosen what is evil. And the end result is the same for us as it was for Adam and Eve: death and all forms of sin that lead to death (see Rom. 6:23).

Let me point out to you two results from the disastrous choice that Adam and Eve made about the fruit of the tree of the knowledge of good and evil.

1. Diverted Attention

First, Eve listened to what the devil had to say to her about the fruit itself. The devil diverted her attention from whatever it was that Eve was doing. He called her attention to the tree and its fruit. The Bible tells us the devil came to her in the guise of a beautiful and subtle serpent and said to her, "Hath God said, Ye shall not eat of every tree of the garden?" (Gen. 3:1). There's no indication that Eve had given much thought to the tree before the devil asked her this question. There's no record that she longed for it or had any curiosity about it. She certainly didn't crave it, because she had never tasted it!

In many ways, the devil uses this same tactic today. He calls our attention to how beautiful and refreshing certain foods and beverages appear. It's difficult to go through a day without seeing enticing food and beverage commercials on billboards, on television, and in magazines. Foods are presented in the most tempting ways in stores, restaurants, and on menus. The devil says the same thing to us he said to Eve: "Has God really said you can't have a bite of this?"

A woman once said to me, "If there's a piece of pie in my house, it calls out to me. It says to me, even in the middle of night, 'Eat me. Come eat me.' I can't resist."

Now I'm certainly not linking the devil to a piece of pie, but I am saying this: the devil will always call your attention repeatedly to the thing that is harmful for you, but he will do it in a way that makes you feel deprived if you don't indulge in eating, drinking, or partaking of what is harmful. The implication of the devil is always: "This is so good. Has God really said you can't have any of this good thing?"

Never forget that the fruit of the tree of the knowledge of good and evil was the knowledge of good and evil. There was an element of good in that fruit, not just evil. The devil told Eve specifically that the fruit of the tree was "good for food, and that it was pleasant to the eyes" (Gen. 3:6). All Eve had to do was look to see that the fruit was pleasant. She made a bad assumption, however, that what was visually pleasant would also be "good for food." In that, the devil was very wrong!

What about us? There's an element of good in foods and substances that are ultimately bad for us, even if it's just the good appearance, smell, or taste. Have you ever noticed how beautiful all the colored and distinctly shaped bottles look in a bar? Those bottles always seem lighted in just the right way to make them look very special, very festive, very appealing. Many foods are pleasant to the eyes. Many drinks are presented in ways that make them appear pleasing. We buy into the lie that what is pleasing is also nutritious and beneficial.

Fasting calls us to turn away from food. Fasting calls us to redivert our attention back to the things of God and His commandments. Fasting calls us to face and overcome the devil's call: "Has God really said you can't have this?" Fasting calls us to abstain from all things harmful for us, and in most cases, from all food for a period of time. The devil's insistent question is likely to become very loud in our minds as we begin a fast: "Has God really said you can't eat? Not anything? Not the things you love the most? Has God really called you to fast—to abstain totally from this thing that you have labeled as 'good'?"

Our answer must be a firm "Yes! God has called me to fast. He has called me to give my full attention to Him and to His commandments. He has called me to obey Him fully in all things. And God has called me to say no to you, devil!"

2. Temptations Toward False Benefits

Eve listened to what the devil had to say to her about the benefits of eating what God had prohibited. The devil always points out the would-be and usually short-term benefits of sin. Many substances that are ultimately harmful for us taste good or feel good or bring pleasure. In some cases, the partaking of the substance makes us feel like adults, feel accepted by others, or feel more powerful and in greater control. Some people say about certain foods and substances that they "give me quick energy," "make me more alert," or "help me relax."

The devil told Eve that the fruit from the tree of the knowledge of good and evil would make her wise—she would be as a "god," knowing good and evil.

In the short term, the devil was right. Eve suddenly had a knowledge of evil. She really knew in her own experience as a human being that evil existed. This was the first time in her life she had ever known the contrast—up to that point, all things had been good.

What the devil failed to mention to Eve was the ultimate consequence that God had associated with eating of this fruit: "You shall surely die." The devil failed to mention any downside to her disobedience. In fact, he dismissed God's consequences with a sarcastic question.

The devil comes at us the same way. The devil never tells us that drinking alcohol can make a person an alcoholic. He never tells a person that smoking cigarettes can cause him or her to have lung cancer. He never tells a person that eating too much of the wrong foods can lead to chronic illness and premature death. The devil points out only short-term benefits, never long-term disasters.

When we fast, we are suddenly aware once again of what is good and evil. We have a heightened awareness not only of God's goodness and of God's commandments, but of the evil that abounds in the world around us.

A man once said to me about fasting, "It seems that when I fast the world seems much more black and white, at least for a period of time. I see right and wrong much more clearly. I see good and bad, blessings and cursings, benefits and negative consequences, what is godly and what is ungodly. I am much more discerning about what lines up with God's commandments and what falls into the category of 'man's commands.'"

I asked him what happened after he stopped fasting. He laughed and said, "I am still very clear on these things, but there's also a time after I end fasting that the whole world seems more vivid and more colorful than ever before. I can distinguish tastes again. The sky seems bluer than before. The air seems crisper in the mountains. All of my senses seem to be heightened toward what is God's creation—which is always good— and what is man's invention—which very often has an element of evil to it."

Those who fast often experience greater discernment of good and evil. In fact, it seems to be a major by-product of fasting. God seems to give us an opportunity as we fast to take a look again at our lives and the world around us and to discern what is good and what is evil.

WHAT JESUS TAUGHT ABOUT FASTING

Most Christians I meet are concerned primarily with what Jesus taught about fasting. We should perhaps begin with what He did not teach. Jesus did not give any regulations related to how long or how often His followers should fast. He did, however, teach His followers two general principles related to fasting, and He did say that His followers would fast.

The Bible tells us that the disciples of John the Baptist came to Jesus and asked, "Why do we and the Pharisees fast oft, but thy disciples fast not?" And Jesus said to them, "Can the children of the bridechamber mourn, as long as the bridegroom is with them? But the days will come, when the bridegroom shall be taken from them, and then shall they fast" (Matt. 9:14–15).

Jesus was pointing toward two key principles related to fasting in this brief statement. First, He was stating that fasting is rooted in an expression of *sorrow*. We see this throughout the Old Testament when those who fasted tore their garments and put on sackcloth and ashes. These were outward, visible, tangible signs that the person fasting felt as if his heart had been torn from his body, just as his garments were torn. Sackcloth was very rough and uncomfortable—it was a sign that the person fasting was in discomfort of some kind, spiritually as well as in other ways. The ashes referred to loss and at times, death—they were a sign that the person was struggling with the loss of something or someone precious and valuable and beloved. (We'll talk more about sorrow later in the chapter.)

The disciples who were close to Jesus at the time of His

earthly ministry could not fast because Jesus manifested such joy, purpose, love, and the saving power of God to those who came into contact with Him. Demons fled. Sickness vanished. The lame walked and the blind saw. There was no sorrow whatsoever associated with Jesus, and no manifestations of sorrow were appropriate for those living in His presence.

Second, Jesus pointed to a time when His disciples would fast. They would fast when they were troubled in spirit . . . when they did not see the miracle-producing power of God manifested through their ministries . . . when they did not see souls saved at the preaching of the gospel . . . when they were feeling weak in spirit, mind, emotions, or body . . . when they were feeling estranged from their heavenly Father . . . and when they were grieving the persecution of their fellow believers.

Jesus told His disciples that they would need to fast and pray in order to discern God's will and God's methods, and that they would need to fast and pray in order to have the power of God resident in them to meet and overcome satanic attacks and cases of demon possession.

In later cases in the New Testament in which we read of Christian men and women fasting, no reference is given, in most cases, to how long the people fasted or by what method. We can conclude that they fasted according to the way the Lord directed them to fast. And what was true for them is true for us also: we are to fast as the Spirit leads us to fast—the method, time, and *purposes* of the fast are to be of His choosing.

HEARTFELT SINCERITY AND GOD'S REWARD

I stated earlier that Jesus gave His disciples two general principles about fasting. This is what He said:

Moreover when ye fast, be not, as the hypocrites, of a sad countenance: for they disfigure their faces, that they may appear unto men to fast. Verily I say unto you, They have their reward. But thou, when thou fastest, anoint thine head, and wash thy face; that thou appear not unto men to fast, but unto thy Father which is in secret: and thy Father, which seeth in secret, shall reward thee openly. (Matthew 6:16–18)

Notice that in this passage Jesus said, "When ye fast" (v. 16). Again, Jesus did not command fasting but He recognized that His disciples would fast.

Jesus clearly taught His disciples that fasting was to be a very private matter between a person and the Lord. This does not mean that a group of people cannot agree together to fast and pray about a particular matter, or that a church cannot declare a time of fasting and prayer in order to call people to a renewed relationship with the Lord.

The disciples were taught that they should appear *to the world* as if they were not fasting. They were not to call attention to their fasting in hopes of winning recognition or sympathy from other people. Most of the people who fasted in Jesus' day walked with bowed heads and sad expressions, often putting ashes on their heads and as a result, ashes on their faces. They were trying to appear righteous. Jesus said, "That will work! People will think you are righteous if you do that. But it is only people who will reward that behavior. God doesn't."

Jesus taught that people were to fast and pray as a personal and private spiritual discipline before the Lord.

Jesus also taught, however, a second principle and it was this: what the Father sees in secret, He rewards openly. Jesus linked fasting with benefit—and it was a benefit that would have outward, visible, tangible results.

SENSING THE HOLY SPIRIT'S CALL TO FAST

The New Testament does not tell us that Jesus taught His followers to fast and pray during a certain season on the calendar or on a certain date every year. Jesus, however, kept the feasts and fast days of the Jews while He was on earth, and He certainly must have kept the fast day that the Jews called the Day of Atonement.

On that one day of the year—usually in September on our calendar—the Jews fasted, prayed, and sacrificed two animals to the Lord. One animal was a blood sacrifice, with the blood sprinkled on the ark of the covenant in the holy of holies so that God would roll back the sins of the Jews and not punish them. The other animal had hands laid upon it—signifying the transfer of the guilt of the people—and was sent away to die in the wilderness. God commanded this fast day and all the rituals associated with it (Lev. 16).

But Jesus became our Atonement sacrificed on the cross. It was His shed blood that became the blood sacrifice for our sins. He absorbed the guilt and shame associated with our sins. The Bible tells us that the sacrifice He made was "once for all" (Heb. 10:10).

As a sign of this, the veil that separated the holy of holies from the rest of the temple was supernaturally divided into two pieces at the time Jesus died on the cross. There was no more need for the rituals associated with the Day of Atonement and the Passover Feast after Jesus was crucified and rose from the dead.

So when is a Christian to fast? When the Holy Spirit prompts a Christian to fast! Nearly always, the Holy Spirit prompts a person to fast by giving him or her a sense that the time has come to quit living with a problem. Sometimes the problem has an element of sorrow to it—there's pain, grief, disappointment, or some form of emotional or physical distress.

Jesus indicated His disciples would fast when the Bridegroom was no longer with them—certainly at that time, after walking so closely with the Lord, they would be sorrowful in spirit.

What I have seen in my years of ministry is that most people have sorrow in their lives. In fact, most people walking around today with smiles on their faces have hidden aches in their hearts. They have just learned to push them down and go on with their lives. They have learned to put on a smile and to say "Fine" when people ask them how they are. They have grown accustomed to *tolerating* a certain degree of sadness, disappointment, sorrow, pain, grief, and hurting in their lives.

God never called His people to a lifelong pattern of sorrow. Throughout the Bible we find that God called His people to experience joy and to be people who would speak joy into the world! We praise with joy. We encourage with joy. We teach with joy. We love with joy. We minister with joy so we can bring other people into the joy of the Lord. We are to be people of joy!

God's purpose for us is joy, and because He desires to produce joy in us, God moves toward us in a very direct way when He sees us weighed down, slowed down, or pressed down by sorrow. In order to draw us to a time of fasting and prayer, the Holy Spirit often allows us to feel our sorrow in more acute ways.

THE INCREASE OF SORROW

What is it that increases feelings of sorrow in our lives? A number of things produce sorrow in our hearts, but these four are among the most common:

1. Impending Doom

The danger might be actual, potential, or perceived. When the people of Moab and other neighboring tribes threatened Jehoshaphat, he called a fast (2 Chron. 20:3). Jehoiakim proclaimed a fast as a sign of penitence to avoid God's punishment (Jer. 36:9). In the days of Esther, the Jews in Shushan fasted when they heard of Haman's plot against them (Est. 4:3). The prophet Joel fasted when faced with a plague of locusts (Joel 1:14, 2:15). Ezra fasted as he prepared for what he perceived to be a dangerous journey to Jerusalem (Ezra 8:21).

2. Sin

Sin, and especially a habit of sin, grieves the Holy Spirit. The guilt we feel when we sin is an expression of grief as well. We know deep within our spirits that we have acted in a way that will bring God's chastisement, and we feel sorrow that our behavior will have negative consequences. Sin is conscious rebellion—it is doing what we know God commands us not to do—and rebellion always separates a person from God's blessings. To be separated from God in any way *should* bring sorrow to a person's heart!

3. Hurtful Habits

There are times when the Holy Spirit allows us to become acutely aware of ways in which we have unknowingly made mistakes. Sometimes these hurtful habits are related to food or other substances we have taken into our bodies—we have injured our health by what we have consumed and by the quantity we have consumed. At times the hurtful habits are emotional or mental—we have fallen into a pattern of responding to life in unhealthy ways.

4. Confusion

At times the Holy Spirit allows us to become acutely aware that we simply do not know our problem or know what to do in response to a specific situation. The situation we are facing may not be negative—it may be the dilemma of choosing between two options that appear to be equally good. It may be at the start of a new ministry—we simply don't know how to begin or where to turn for help. At times the problem is one related to a relationship. We don't understand the motives or behavior of another person who is close to us.

Certainly all of us sense danger at times. All of us sin, develop unhealthy habits, and are confused occasionally. Usually our first response is to cry out to God for help, forgiveness, courage, and/or wisdom to make necessary changes in our lives. In crying out to God, we usually feel God's presence with us and we begin to trust God in a renewed way to help us face or overcome the danger, repent of the sin and make new godly choices in our lives, change our habits, or seek out the knowledge and understanding we need to do what God commands us to do.

But . . . there are times when the heavens seem to be shut to us.

God's answers don't seem to come.

We can't seem to find our way.

We can't seem to exert enough willpower to do what we know we should do.

We can't seem to break the power of an addiction or to resolve the difficulties in a relationship.

We sense deep within that we need to do *more* to put ourselves in a position to hear from God and to experience the power and presence of God in our lives. It is in those times that the Holy Spirit very likely is calling us to pray and fast.

WHEN THINGS ARE GOING BADLY

One of the most unusual times of fasting is recorded in the book of Judges. This fast came at a time when things were going very badly for eleven of the tribes of Israel.

We are told in Judges 19–20 the story of a man who was supposed to have been a priest, although there is no indication that he was really a man of God. This was a time in the history of Israel in which "every man did that which was right in his own eyes" (Judg. 17:6). People were doing their own thing, instead of doing God's thing.

This particular priest had a concubine who went to visit her father. She was away for four months. When the priest went to take her back to their home in Bethlehem, he stayed for several days with his concubine's father. The two men drank a great deal. Then the priest and his concubine started back to Bethlehem. They entered a town of the Benjaminites and had difficulty finding lodging. Finally a man invited them to stay the night. The Benjaminites were well known for their cruelty and immorality. The priest gave the men access to his concubine for the night. They abused her all night and then left her dead on the doorstep.

When the priest was ready to leave the following morning, he found his concubine dead. He cut her body into twelve pieces and sent one section of her body to each tribe of Israel. What a grisly and terrible story this is! I can't begin to imagine opening a package and finding a piece of someone's body in it. The priest sent a message with his bloody package: "This is what the Benjaminites have done to my concubine!" So the other tribes sent a message to the Benjaminites, saying, "Give us those men so we can punish them." The Benjaminites refused.

The eleven other tribes of Israel joined together to take on the Benjaminites. As an interesting fact, the Benjaminites had seven hundred left-handed men in their army and "every one could sling stones at an hair breadth, and not miss" (Judg. 20:16). The Benjaminites ended up winning two battles, one in which twenty-two thousand men were killed!

When I first studied this passage in the book of Judges I thought this seemed terribly unfair. I thought, *God, the other tribes were right! Why did You let the Benjaminites win?* The Bible does not give us a direct answer to that question, but the more I have studied this passage, the more I have concluded the reason may have been that the other eleven tribes of Israel had moved so far away from God that the powers of darkness had overwhelmed the nation. Those eleven tribes apparently were moving against Benjamin totally according to their own understanding of what was right. They had no reliance upon God and they had failed to seek God diligently before they went into this battle against one of their own. It was only when the "children of Israel arose, and went up to the house of God, and asked counsel of God" that the tide of war began to turn (Judg. 20:18).

When things are definitely not going our way—when they aren't moving in the direction of righteousness that we believe is in accordance with God's command—we need to find out why! In those times, we should never get together in groups and exchange ideas out of our human knowledge and understanding. We need to have God's opinion! If ever there is a good time for prayer and fasting, it is when we appear to be losing battles to the devil that we believe we should be winning according to God's promises and commandments.

Finally we read:

> Then all the children of Israel, and all the people, went up, and came unto the house of God, and wept, and sat there before the LORD, and fasted that day until even, and offered burnt offerings and peace offerings before the LORD. And the children of Israel enquired of the LORD, (for the ark of the covenant of God was there in those days, and Phinehas, the son of Eleazar, the son of Aaron, stood before it in those days,) saying, Shall I yet again go out to battle against the children of Benjamin my brother, or shall I cease? And the LORD said, Go up; for tomorrow I will deliver them into thine hand." (Judges 20:26–28)

Anytime things are going badly in your life . . . when you are faced with great pain, trouble, or difficulty . . . when you are in a decision-making crisis . . . when you don't know what to do . . . ask the Holy Spirit if He is leading you to a time of praying and fasting.

NEED FOR A TIME SET APART

In addition to a growing inner sense of burden, heaviness, or sorrow, we often have a growing feeling that we need to make a break with the current way of doing things, and in turn, make a new start. This, too, is a way in which the Holy Spirit leads us to fast as we pray.

A period of fasting sends a signal to your own body, soul, and spirit that you are not conducting your life in a "business as usual" manner. You are declaring an intermission, of sorts, between the way things have been and the way you desire things to be. You are setting aside a period of time to devote yourself more intensely and fervently to the Lord in a sacrificial way.

The apostle Paul wrote to the Romans that they were to present their bodies as a "living sacrifice" (Rom. 12:1). In many ways, a time of fasting is a time of personal sacrifice. A sacrifice is something we give to the Lord completely—never to receive it back again. The food that you give up in a time of fasting is food that you will never eat. The time that you give up in praying is time that you will never experience again. The offering of your praise and thanksgiving to the Lord takes your intention, your energy, your effort—you are giving to the Lord the very essence of what makes you *you*. You are giving up to Him your identity, your life.

A time of fasting is a way of saying to the Lord, "If You do not act, Lord, to help me, I will perish. My life and my times are in Your hand."

Certainly when we are faced with danger, we often feel this way. Unless the Lord acts, we may very well lose our lives or a valuable aspect of our lives.

Certainly when we are confronting our own sin or unhealthy habits, we feel this way. Without God's help, we are on a slippery slope to our own demise. Unless we receive the Lord's assistance, we are likely to fall into a miry pit.

Certainly when we are confronting our own confusion, we feel this way. Without God's wisdom, we will not succeed. Our marriages will fail, our businesses will fail, our ministries will fail.

Fasting is moving away from the things of this world in order to draw closer to God, and in drawing closer to God, to receive from God the things we need most:

- A renewed sense of trust, and an increase of faith.
- Forgiveness and restoration.
- Health and wholeness.
- Wisdom and understanding.

A person who has those four things in his or her life—in abundance—is a person who has joy, not sorrow. A person who is trusting God, fully forgiven, healthy and vibrant, knowing where he is going with a direction and passion from the Lord to accomplish a mission: that is a person who experiences great confidence. Such a person feels a closeness to the Lord, a nearness of the Bridegroom that defies all logic or rationality. Outward circumstances may not be different, situations may not yet have changed, danger may still exist, but the person who walks in trust, faith, forgiveness, healing, and wisdom is a person who is eager to face whatever life may bring with a confidence that God can and will work all things to that person's good (Rom. 8:28).

AN EXPECTANCY THAT GOD WILL ACT

Part of the way we know that the Holy Spirit is leading us to a fast is a sense of mystery. Even though we might feel great sorrow and sense that we need to pull away from the world for a season, we nearly always have a sense that now is the time for us to fast and pray because God desires to do something very good in our lives! We have an expectancy that God is going to make Himself known in a very powerful and personal way.

The person who begins to fast and pray may feel fear about impending dangers, but he will also feel that God desires to show Himself strong in the situation and that God desires to deliver.

The person who begins to fast and pray may feel great guilt or sorrow over sin, but he will also feel that God desires to forgive and to cleanse and to restore.

The person who begins to fast and pray may feel that he has become the victim of his own mistakes and errors in allowing certain habits to take root in his life, but he will also feel that God desires to free him from past habits and to guide and help him develop new habits that will lead to wholeness.

The person who begins to fast and pray may feel confused and even depressed in his confusion, but he will also feel hope that God is going to cause the confusion and depression to lift so the person can see with a renewed vision what God has planned for the future.

Read again what the Lord said through the prophet Jeremiah:

> For I know the thoughts that I think toward you, saith the LORD, thoughts of peace, and not of evil, to give you an expected end. Then shall ye call upon me, and ye shall go and pray unto me, and I will hearken unto you. And ye shall seek me, and find me, when ye shall search for me with all your heart. And I will be found of you, saith the LORD; . . . and I will bring you again into the place whence I caused you to be carried away captive. (Jeremiah 29:11–14)

God has something wonderful for us. He has a break-through for our lives. He does not call us to fast and pray so that we can die, but so that we can experience a newness of life. He calls us to a time of fasting and prayer so that we might give up everything that keeps us from experiencing the abundant life He has for us. He calls us to fast and pray so that we can experience His peace and move into the future that He has already prepared for us—a future in which those things that have held us captive no longer do so! We will no longer be the victim of enemy assaults, sin's consequences, poor health, or dark confusion.

The Holy Spirit leads us to fast and pray so that we might transition from the way we have been living to a new and higher way of living.

2

HOW FASTING AND PRAYER ARE LINKED

Most Christians agree that prayer is powerful. In fact, nobody I know—Christian or unbeliever—is willing to say that prayer is unproductive or of no importance. Even those who say they don't particularly "believe" in prayer want a believing person to pray if they become sick or experience a great need or tragedy in their lives! People around the world, in every culture and throughout the ages, have believed in the usefulness of expressing oneself to God—of praising and worshiping God, of thanking God, and of voicing prayer requests to God. Even people who don't particularly believe in the *power* of prayer tend to admit that prayer has value and is important as part of a person's spiritual life and expression.

THE NATURE OF PRAYER

Prayer is communicating with God. Prayer is generally spoken. Prayers can originate in the mind, the soul, and the spirit. We ask God for things we perceive we *need* on the basis of what we see, sense, and think. We ask God for things we *desire* on the basis of our innermost feelings, wants, and hopes. We also are commanded in the Bible to pray for the *deepest longings* of our eternal spirits—to pray for those things that are ours to claim and receive in the spiritual realm, both now and for all eternity. The deepest prayers are those spoken from the spirit of a person by the inspiration and power of the Holy Spirit. The Bible teaches us to pray with the Spirit, and with understanding (1 Cor. 14:15).

Prayer is primarily a spiritual activity. For Christians especially, prayer does not require a particular location or position of the body. A person can pray lying down, kneeling, sitting, standing up, and even driving a car or folding clothes. A person can pray anyplace—at home, at church, at work. A person does not need to put on special clothing or take off makeup or put on a scowl or frown to pray. Neither does a person need to use "thee" and "thou" language.

The Bible tells us that when we pray, God looks on the *heart*: "The LORD seeth not as man seeth; for man looketh on the outward appearance, but the LORD looketh on the heart" (1 Sam. 16:7).

A Focus on God, Eternity, and All Things Spiritual

Prayer shifts our focus away from the routines and daily grind of this world toward things that are eternal. It shifts the focus away from our problems and on to God's answers. It shifts our preoccupation with the current problem or crisis toward those things that bring God's answers and God's help.

Praise and thanksgiving are definitely among the ways in which prayer refocuses our lives spiritually. The Bible commands us to give thanks. The apostle Paul wrote, "In every thing by prayer and supplication with thanksgiving let your requests be made known unto God" (Phil. 4:6).

We are to thank God for all that He has given to us and done for us in the past, all that He is giving to us and doing for us in the present, and all that we believe He is going to give to us and do for us in the future according to the promises of His Word. That's a lot for which to give thanks! In fact, you could spend the rest of your life just giving thanks to the Lord, and you'd find that the more you did so, the more reasons you had to give Him thanks.

The more you thank God for the things He has given to you, the more you begin to see that God is capable of meeting all of your needs. The more you thank Him for His provision, very often you find your desire lessening for more "stuff" of this world. The more you thank God for how He has protected you and nurtured you in the past, the greater your faith seems to rise to believe for His protection and nurturing in the future! The more you thank God for your salvation, the more you desire to see others saved.

What about praise? We praise God for who He is—not only to us, but who He is by His nature.

We praise God for being our Savior, our Deliverer, our Healer, and for being the Author and Finisher of our faith.

We praise God for being the Balm of Gilead that heals us and for being our Resurrection and Life. We praise God for His always faithful, always loving, patient, forgiving nature. We praise God for His attributes or "fruit" that He is producing in our lives (Gal. 5:22–23). We praise God for being holy, unchanging, just, merciful, and kind.

Just as with thanksgiving, you can never praise God for all that He is because God is infinite! There is no end to praise!

What happens inside you as you praise God—and I mean really *praise* God without any concern for time passing? Something inside you begins to break and be molded more into the likeness of Jesus Christ. Something inside you begins to rise up because you begin to see God as being greater than any problem you have, mightier than any enemy that is coming against you, and more loving than any amount of discouragement, disappointment, or depression you may feel. You begin to catch a glimpse of God's majesty and glory. You begin to see God for how powerful and mighty He truly is!

The more you praise God, the smaller your problems become in comparison to the infinite greatness of God.

The Impact of Praise and Thanksgiving on Our Petitions

The Bible tells us to enter the gates of the Lord with thanksgiving, and to enter His courts with praise (Ps. 100:4). When we enter a time of prayer before the Lord with thanksgiving and praise, very often we find that our petitions become very few and far more focused. We begin to see that our loving and faithful heavenly Father has already provided for us all things that we need and are going to need, and that He has already begun to work all things out for our good (Rom. 8:28). In many cases, thanksgiving and praise build our faith and give us confidence so that we can come before the Lord boldly. In many cases, thanksgiving and praise change the way we think so that our petitions change—and in the vast majority of cases, change so that they are in total alignment with God's will.

Because thanksgiving and praise are a part of prayer, I will also challenge you in the coming chapters to spend time in thanksgiving and praise.

THE NATURE OF FASTING

Fasting deals with the physical nature of you as a person. It addresses the very nature of your physical and material life on this earth.

Prayer is spiritual. Fasting is "natural" or "of the flesh."

Prayer is a spiritual discipline. Fasting is a physical discipline.

Prayer turns a person's eyes toward God. Fasting turns a person's attention away from this world.

Prayer calls a person to focus on those things that are eternal and of greatest importance to God. Fasting calls a person to leave behind—even temporarily—an overriding concern with things that are earthbound and timebound.

Prayer challenges a person to trust God for all things related to eternal life and the deep things of an abundant, spiritual life. Fasting challenges a person to trust God in all things pertaining to the material and physical dimensions of life.

What exactly does it mean to fast? It means to give up or reduce the intake of things that you need to sustain life. In most cases, it means giving up food and liquid *to some degree* and *for some length of time.*

We'll deal with types of fasts later, but for now, the critical concept for you to understand is this: fasting moves you away from a preoccupation with this world—from the time, material, and substance of the earth—even as prayer draws you into a deeper relationship with God Almighty.

"But how," you may be asking, "can fasting move me away from a preoccupation with this world when I am focused on what I am not eating? How can it keep me from being concerned with the flesh when I am hungry all the time?"

Fasting periods very often begin with a great awareness of one's body and of a person's need for food. Fasting often begins with hunger, sometimes with feelings of weakness and deprivation. Fasting can also be a time in which a person experiences some of the adverse effects of the physical body's releasing toxins from the cells of the body—effects that can include some pain as well as intestinal changes. In a later chapter, we will address these physical aspects of fasting and give you ways to begin and end a fast wisely.

Even so, the person who fasts nearly always discovers that after an initial preoccupation with the fact that he is not eating or drinking as usual, he begins to experience some of these feelings:

- A feeling of being cleansed.
- A feeling of being emptied of things that were a burden or a poison.
- A feeling of inner strength at being able to overcome hunger and lack.
- A greater awareness of the intricate and awesome way in which God has made the body.

As these feelings come, and as the fast continues, a person nearly always enters a phase of fasting in which:

- The spiritual becomes far more prominent than the physical.
- The need to eat begins to diminish in importance and a pre-occupation with eating begins to disappear.
- Strength and energy return, often in amazing ways.

It is then that fasting and prayer come together in a powerful combination.

THE COMBINATION OF FASTING AND PRAYER

Two tremendous things happen in the life of a person when fasting and prayer become like the two sides of one coin.

1. A Greater Awareness of Your Human Need

First, the person experiences a greatly heightened awareness of his own limitations, weaknesses, and frailties. Fasting makes a person acutely aware of his dependency upon God's provision—not only on God's provision of food and water, but for all things that are beneficial to an abundant life.

Fasting calls us to confront our weakness as "earthen vessels" (2 Cor. 4:7). We recognize as we fast that there is only so much we can do . . . know . . . accomplish . . . accommodate . . .

take in . . . give out. The Bible tells us that we are a vapor, a wisp, weak, and without any strength of our own. All that we have comes from God. He is the Author and Finisher of our faith, and also of every other aspect of our lives. We are nothing without God at work in us—certainly nothing eternal or of genuine benefit to other people. Fasting brings us to an awareness of our own selves, and with that awareness, a greater understanding of our needs.

Truly to have a breakthrough in your life, you need to identify the real problem or need in your life. That problem may not be the problem you *think* you have as you enter a fast. Very often during a time of fasting and praying, the Lord will reveal a deeper issue in your life. It is that deeper issue that the Lord calls you to address in prayer and with your faithful obedience to His Word.

Let me give you an example. Many people in our nation today have a problem with obesity. They know they are overweight and most admit, "I should lose some weight." For most of those who are overweight, however, there's an underlying issue related to why they are in that condition. That issue might be stress, bad eating habits, or a lack of exercise. But underneath even those issues are likely to be still deeper issues associated with the person's feelings of worthiness. There may be old rejections and hurts that the person covers up with food. The person may have childhood issues of abuse or neglect that he has never addressed. There may be *reasons* for the stress that cause a person to eat too much of the wrong fast foods—issues related to why a person becomes overcommitted, overburdened, or overworked.

Fasting certainly confronts the surface problem of obesity head-on! After all, a person who is fasting isn't eating! But from God's perspective, the real issues that a person needs to address are ones a person will become increasingly aware of as he or she fasts *and prays.* It is in prayer while fasting that the Lord tends to strip away layer upon layer of excuse . . . of justification . . . of procrastination . . . of inattention to the deeper issues that lie in the soul (the mind, emotions, and will) and spirit.

In the final analysis, the person who goes into a fast to overcome an eating problem or an obesity problem—and who is genuinely open to the ways in which God might speak and lead during the fast—is likely to uncover deeper truths about himself or herself. These truths will always relate to how God desires for a person to live in wholeness and in His love, forgiveness, and acceptance. (Before commencing a fast, you should assess your health and consider consulting a health professional.)

Let's deal with another example. You may think divorce is the reason you are embarking on a time of fasting and praying. As you fast with a heart open to God, and as you begin to confront your own weakness as a human being, it is likely the Spirit will lead you to confront some of the issues related to your divorce. The Spirit may cause you to dig deeper into issues related to rejection, anger, a need to control, an insatiable craving for attention and love, an unwillingness to take responsibility for your life, or any one of a number of other issues.

Don't be afraid to dive into the deeper issues of your life as you fast. That's one of the benefits of fasting: you have an opportunity to see and then address those things that stand in the way of your experiencing a real breakthrough in your life!

2. A Greater Awareness of Almighty God

Second, as fasting brings about a greater understanding of our human shortcomings, prayer points us toward the unlimited, all-powerful, and all-wise nature of our loving, eternal God! Prayer opens us up to a greatly heightened awareness of God's presence and glory. Prayer produces in us greater faith and confidence that God is the Problem-Solver of our deepest dilemma!

The weaker you see yourself . . . the stronger the Lord appears.

The more limited you see yourself . . . the more the Lord reveals to you His unlimited power.

The more you realize how bound you are to time and to things of this earth . . . the more the Lord reveals to you the tremendous freedom that He desires for you to experience.

The more clearly you see your problem . . . the more clearly you see that God is not only bigger than your problem, but that He has already provided the answer for your problem. A process unfolds:

- *What is revealed in fasting becomes the focus for prayer.* Fasting brings us to the place of knowing what we must pray about. It gives us clarity and insight and focus.
- *What becomes the focus for prayer becomes the battleground in the spirit realm—the battle that we must fight and win through the Lord Jesus Christ.* When we know the focus for our prayers, we know how to pray, against what to pray, and for what to pray. Our expectancy for God's answer is also brought into sharper focus. We truly know the nature of the miracle that God desires us to have!
- *What is won in the Spirit becomes the victory or the breakthrough that changes us from the inside out.* Spiritual warfare in prayer brings us to a new commitment, a new discipline, a new strength, a new level of faith. The end result is always something better, something greater, something more. Jesus said, "The thief cometh not, but for to steal, and to kill, and to destroy: I am come that they might have life, and that they might have it more abundantly" (John 10:10). The devil always comes to detract from us, take away from us, and diminish us. Jesus came to give us God's abundance: spiritually, mentally, emotionally, relationally, financially, materially. God's abundance covers every area of life. Jesus came to give us more . . . and more . . . and more. He came to give us an overflowing

abundance so that we might be a greater, and greater, and greater blessing to others.

Can you see how fasting and prayer work together? A tremendous blessing awaits those who will do as the Lord commanded: pray and fast.

Fasting and prayer take us out of the downward cycle into spiritual poverty, loss, sickness, brokenness, sin, and decay . . . and turn things around so that we move to an upward cycle into:

- Spiritual riches in Christ Jesus.
- All things we might call gain.
- All aspects of health and wholeness.
- New realms of restoration and reconciliation.
- Righteous living—all things that put us into right standing with God and in right standing to receive God's blessings.
- Life-producing witness and outreach to other people.

What a plan God has for us! Fasting and prayer put us into position to receive all that He desires for us to have and to give.

3

THE SPIRITUAL DISCIPLINE OF FASTING

Seeking God's will must be our highest priority in a time of prayer and fasting. The apostle Paul called the Romans to present their bodies as "living sacrifices, holy and pleasing to God." This, he taught, led to a person's being "transformed by the renewing of [his] mind." And then, Paul said, "you will be able to test and approve what God's will is—his good, pleasing and perfect will" (Rom. 12:1–2 NIV).

The Bible is very clear on the issue of God's will: believers are to know it and obey it. His will should be our highest priority. Jesus said we should pray for God's will to be accomplished here on earth—right now, today—as it is being accomplished in heaven.

On more than one occasion Jesus said in humility to the Father, "Not my will, but Thine be done." Jesus said to His followers, "The Son can do nothing by Himself." Rather, Jesus said, He could "do only what he sees his Father doing, because whatsoever the Father does the Son also does" (John 5:19 NIV).

This, then, is the challenge that we are given as we pray and fast: we are to discern God's will and make a commitment to do it! In the end, we must follow through—discerning and committing are not enough. We must actually obey the will of God and say and do what the Lord has revealed to us we are to say and do.

CONFRONTING OUR OWN SELVES

Fasting calls us to confront these specific things in our lives: our habits, our priorities, and our relationship with the Lord.

Our Habits

As we discern what is good and evil during a time of fasting, we have an opportunity to ask ourselves, *Are the habits in my life ones that produce what is good, godly, and life-producing, or am I engaging in habits that are ultimately harmful to me? Are the habits of my life leading me toward God, or away from God? Are the habits of my life producing health, or are they habits that will eventually lead to sickness, disease, weakness, and even death?*

Recognize as you reevaluate your habits that your habits produce results not only in your life, but in the lives of others around you. The way you eat is likely to be the way you feed your spouse and children. The way you live is likely the lifestyle you are passing to the next generation. The way you worship God is very likely the way others around you will come to worship God. Ask yourself, *Are the habits of my life helpful or hurtful to those around me?*

Very few of us like to confront our habits. Habits are the comfortable ruts that we've dug for ourselves. It's easier to continue to walk forward in a rut than to make a change. New habits are difficult to develop.

Let me encourage you in this: You *can* learn new habits. You *can* change bad habits into good habits. You *can* turn your life away from what is harmful or death-producing and begin to move toward what is beneficial and life-producing.

Furthermore, God will help you make the change toward new, good habits if you ask for His help! God does not want you to be trapped in a downward spiral of bad habits. He wants you to succeed in developing healthy habits that give you even more energy, strength, and vitality as His beloved child! Ask for God's discernment about which habits you need to change, which you need to get rid of, and which you need to adopt or add to your life. Ask for His help in making these changes.

Our Priorities

As we discern what is good and evil during a time of fasting, we also have an opportunity to ask ourselves: *Am I devoting the best of my talents, abilities, time, and money to things that truly are good and that produce good in this world?*

Some activities aren't bad as much as they are meaningless. They won't matter a hundred years from now. They may not cause harm to anybody, but they don't produce a heavenly reward. They may not be evil, but neither do they give a person a deep feeling of satisfaction and fulfillment.

God calls us to live productive, high-quality, beneficial lives. He calls us to do good in this world. The prophet Micah declared this word of the Lord: "What doth the LORD require of thee, but to do justly, and to love mercy, and to walk humbly with thy God?" (Mic. 6:8).

To walk humbly before God refers to our habits . . . our lifestyles . . . our ways of living out the commandments of God. To "do justly" and to "love mercy" refer more to our priorities. God calls each of us to make a decision about how we will "love mercy"—in other words, how much we will value giving to others and showing kindness to others. The greatest act of kindness, of course, is to lead another person to the Lord. We have to decide how we will support and be part of ministries that reach out to the lost, sick, and needy around the world. We have to decide how high on our priority list are activities that extend God's love, mercy, and salvation to others.

God calls us to make a decision about how we will "do

justly"—in other words, where and when we will take a stand
for what is right. We need to decide how much of our time, effort, and resources we will give to those causes and issues that
uphold God's commandments and help to create and sustain a
godly, moral society. We have to decide how high on our priority list are activities and associations that proclaim God's truth
and teach God's Word to all nations (Matt. 28:19).

A time of fasting gives us pause to reflect upon our priorities and to make adjustments and new commitments about how
we will spend the time, talents, and resources that God has put
into our hands.

One person said to me after a time of fasting, "I kept thinking
about how much time and energy I normally spend in relationship
to food. There's not only the eating of food, but the shopping for
food, preparing food, and cleaning up after cooking meals. I fig-
ured there were at least ten hours a week that I spent making shopping lists, grocery shopping, driving to the grocery store as well as
to our favorite delicatessens and specialty food stores, cooking,
and cleaning up—and probably about five to seven more hours
driving to restaurants, waiting for a table in restaurants, and eating
in restaurants—as well as time in drive-through lanes at fast-food
restaurants. In all I was probably spending close to twenty weeks a
year on food-related activities."

"That's a lot," I said.

She continued, "Then I thought about how much money I
spent on food. I kept track for one month. I had thought I was
spending only about four hundred dollars for our family of
four, but when I added up all the restaurant charges, fast food
slips, and grocery receipts, I discovered we were spending close
to six hundred dollars on food."

"What did you do?" I asked.

"I talked it over with my husband and we prayed about what
changes we should make in our lives. We both agreed we were
spending way too much time and money on feeding ourselves.

We made several adjustments about how we spend our time and money, and we cut both our food-related time and our food-related budgets just about in half."

I asked, "What did that mean to your lives?"

"We not only decided to be better stewards of our food money and food time, but we decided that the ten hours a week that we were not spending on food-related activities we would spend in ministry as a family—either individually or together. We each devoted more time to prayer, Bible study, and to helping with various ministries at the church. We were already tithing, but we decided that the money we saved on food we would split three ways—one-third of the saved amount went as an offering to the Lord's work, one-third went into savings, and one-third went into a special account for taking our entire family on a mission trip that our church sponsored."

The woman paused and then said what so many people have said to me through the years, "Marilyn, fasting changed our lives. It changed my life individually. It changed my husband's life. It changed the life of each of my children."

Our Relationship with the Lord

Fasting calls us to reevaluate and renew our relationship with the Lord. Very often people who are fasting feel a strong conviction that they have not been loving the Lord with their whole hearts, souls, and minds (Matt. 22:37). They feel convicted to spend more time reading and studying their Bibles. They feel compelled to spend more time in prayer—not just in short spurts of prayer, but in prolonged seasons of offering thanksgiving and praise to the Lord, interceding for their loved ones and for lost souls to be saved. They feel a renewed commitment to hearing what God might say to them regarding ways in which they are to tell others about Jesus and to become involved in outreach ministries.

A woman came to me during a fast time and said, "I thought

I was just giving up food in this fast, but I discovered something a few days ago."

"What was that?" I asked.

"I discovered that I no longer feel like tuning in certain programs on television or listening to certain types of music. Watching some of the TV programs I had been watching suddenly seemed very *unimportant*. In fact, they seemed like a total waste of my time. I realized that I had started listening to some things on radio and television that were upholding values that are not at all in line with God's Word. I felt very convicted about them."

"What did you do?"

She continued, "I've been spending more time reading—and especially reading the Bible and books that are written by Christian authors. I've been spending more time in silence, or with quiet praise music in the background at home. When I'm in my car, I listen to soothing praise tapes. It's been wonderful. I have much more peace in my life and feel much less stressed out at the end of a day. I had thought fasting would be very stressful—not eating, feeling hungry and exhausted. But instead, I have felt rejuvenated and calm and. . . ."

She seemed to struggle to find the word and finally she said, "More centered. Yes, more centered on the Lord and on things that really matter."

Fasting separates us, in many ways, from the routines and pressures of this world. It sets us apart so we can spend time with the Lord.

SPENDING TIME WITH THE LORD

Certainly one of the foremost reasons to fast is to spend more time in prayer. When God calls people to pray, very often He calls them to fast and pray so that there is no interruption in their prayer time. One person once said, "To me, the ideal approach to fasting is to spend so much time in prayer, to be so devoted to interceding in prayer, that I simply forget to eat. I become so involved in the need I must take to the Lord that food becomes unimportant."

In 1 Corinthians 7, the apostle Paul wrote that a husband and wife should not abstain from having sexual relations "except it be with consent for a time, that ye may give yourselves to fasting and prayer" (1 Cor. 7:5). Paul considered fasting and prayer a means of putting the things of God before other normal earthly activities, not only eating in this case, but also sexual activity.

An Earnest Desire to Know God's Plan and Purposes

There are times and situations in which fasting is a manifestation of a person's earnestness before God to the exclusion of all other activities. Nearly always this earnestness is born of a desire to know more clearly God's plan and purposes and, if possible, to make a difference through prayer.

This certainly was true in the life of King David.

After David committed adultery with Bathsheba, Uriah's wife, and then ordered Uriah to the front lines of battle where he was killed, David married Bathsheba and she conceived a child. The prophet Nathan came to David to confront him about his sin and to express God's displeasure about what David had done. David said to Nathan with repentant sorrow, "I have sinned against the LORD." Nathan responded with these words from the Lord: "The LORD also hath put away thy sin; thou shalt not die. Howbeit, because by this deed thou hast given great occasion to the enemies of the LORD to blaspheme, the child also that is born unto thee shall surely die" (2 Sam. 12:13–14).

David responded to this visit from Nathan by beseeching God for the child and by fasting. The Bible tells us that he "went in, and lay all night upon the earth" and that he would not rise up or eat for seven days (2 Sam. 12:16). On the seventh day, the child died and it was only then that David arose, washed and anointed himself, changed his clothes, and went to the house of the Lord to worship God. After he had worshiped, he returned home and ate.

David's servants asked him, "What thing is this that thou hast done? Thou didst fast and weep for the child, while it was alive; but when the child was dead, thou didst rise and eat bread" (2 Sam. 12:21). From their perspective, David had done just the opposite of what other people did. Many people fast when they are grieving and sorrowful—they just don't feel like eating. They pray and work and go to doctors' appointments and do everything they know to do when someone they love is sick—rarely do they lie facedown on the ground and refuse to move because they are so consumed by their desire to pray and intercede for the healing of their loved one.

David replied, "While the child was yet alive, I fasted and wept: for I said, Who can tell whether GOD will be gracious to me, that the child may live? But now he is dead, wherefore should I fast? Can I bring him back again? I shall go to him, but he shall not return to me" (2 Sam. 12:22–23).

David showed us by his example what it means to fast in order to be 100 percent devoted to intercession. Nothing mattered to David at that time other than praying for the life of his infant son. Eating, bathing, changing clothes—all of these normal routines disappeared and in their place, David *prayed*.

One of the most outstanding testimonies I have ever heard about fasting was from a woman in Cincinnati, Ohio. Her son had gone to his mother's homeland of Switzerland to study, and while he was attending a well-known university there, he became very ill. He was not able to eat for a week. Finally a professor said to him, "You have to go to a doctor. Your skin is yellow and you are extremely thin."

The young man went to several physicians, who checked him thoroughly and told him he had a kind of poisoning that was in some way related to food he had eaten. They could do nothing medically for his condition, and they predicted he would die from the poisoning in a short period of time.

This young man called his mother and she immediately flew over to Switzerland. She stayed with her family there but said to them, "Don't ask me to come out of my room. I will come out once or twice a day. I will be fasting until my son gives a positive report." At the time, her son was in the hospital dying.

This mother fasted for seven days, each day coming out several times only to ask about her son's condition. She did not go to see him but simply fasted and prayed in the room at her relative's home. At the end of seven days she received a report from her son's physicians that he was better. The physicians could not understand why! Within a few days, she was able to take her son back to the United States with her. Physicians in the United States thoroughly checked him out and they said they had no idea what he had contracted in Switzerland, but he certainly had received a miracle healing. Fasting and prayer had broken the bonds of illness in this boy's life!

The situation in David's life did not turn out as well—and certainly did not turn out as David had desired. David recognized, however, that the situation had turned out as God desired. David did not have his will in this, but he did have a clear manifestation of God's will. He had poured out his petitions before God for an entire week, not ceasing in his pleas before God. But when God's will had become clear in the matter, David accepted God's will and did not reject it, deny it, or become angry with God. No . . . David cleaned himself up, put on fresh clothes, and went to worship God.

In those days, the place of worship was a tabernacle that David had commanded to be built prior to the building of the temple by Solomon. This tabernacle was an open-air structure with tent-like fabric panels in a large circle around the ark of the covenant. Priests made peace offerings and burnt sacrifices before the Lord there, but mostly, this tabernacle was a place in which singers and musicians offered twenty-four-hour praise before the Lord.

David himself had set the pattern of praise for this tabernacle. He had ordered certain priests to play harps, cymbals, and trumpets to accompany praise songs. David himself had offered the first praise song to God in that place, and it became the pattern for the praise that priests offered continually there.

In going to worship God, David went to sing praises and to play instruments before the Lord that both he and the priests knew well. Let me remind you of part of what David had taught the priests to sing in the tabernacle:

> Give unto the LORD, ye kindreds of the people, give unto the LORD glory and strength.
> Give unto the LORD the glory due unto his name: bring an offering, and come before him: worship the LORD in the beauty of holiness.
> . . . O give thanks unto the LORD; for he is good; for his mercy endureth for ever.
> . . . Blessed be the LORD God of Israel for ever and ever. (1 Chronicles 16:28–29, 34, 36)

In going to worship the Lord after fasting and prayer, David was saying, in essence, "God, You are God! Your will has been done. To You belongs all majesty and authority and power and dominion now and forever."

Putting God First

Let me remind you of two other incidents in the Bible in which fasting and prayer were a manifestation that a person or group was putting God first, before all other normal earthly activities. In both cases, the outcome was a manifestation of God's will toward those who fasted and prayed.

In Acts 10, a Roman centurion by the name of Cornelius

was fasting and praying to know God in a fuller and deeper way. It was while he was fasting and praying that God spoke through a vision to Peter that he was to go to Cornelius and preach to him about Jesus. Fasting and prayer brought about the conversion of all who heard Peter preach in Cornelius's house—and through that experience, the gospel was opened up to Gentiles around the world! It was by fasting and prayer, as well as the giving of alms, that Cornelius put God first.

In Acts 13, the church at Antioch responded to the Holy Spirit's command to "separate" Barnabas and Saul "for the work whereunto I have called them." How did the church respond to this word from the Lord? They "fasted and prayed, and laid their hands on them" and then sent them out to preach the gospel on a major missionary journey (Acts 13:2–3). The church fasted and prayed to hear from God and to obey God fully. They received direction as they fasted and prayed about what it meant to "separate" these two men for a special task.

One year after I began my personal discipline of fasting seven meals a week, I felt led of the Lord to pray over the continents of the earth and over each nation by name. It was not long after that God began to open up many of these nations for crusades and special speaking engagements. One of these nations over which I prayed as I fasted was Pakistan. We have had four crusades in Pakistan and are preparing for a fifth. I strongly believe it was prayer and fasting that first opened that door.

Sudan is another nation in which we have been able to hold a crusade. I was told by event organizers that, to their knowledge, no Christian preaching and teaching crusade had ever been conducted in Khartoum, the capital of Sudan, prior to our going there. We held the meeting on the polo grounds, and the vast majority of people who attended were Muslim. Prior to our going, a twelve-year-old girl had a dream about three dark rings around the sun. She told her pastor about this, and he, in turn, told me. He had no idea what the dream meant, nor did I, but I saw the dream come to pass.

The first day of our Ministry Training School in Khartoum, a dark ring appeared around the sun. The people began to ululate—the word for a high trilling sound the people there make with their tongues. This is what many Africans do when they get excited. We had no idea what was happening at first, but Sudanese Christians told us the people saw this dark ring around the sun as a sign from God.

The following afternoon at the crusade service the people stood and began to run down the polo grounds, ululating and falling on their faces. Some of our staff asked what was happening and they said, "We just saw Jesus in the sun! Look at the sun!" Again, there was a dark ring around the sun. That day I didn't preach but rather gave an altar call and people rushed forward to receive Jesus. We had an unusual manifestation of healings and miracles. The next day—the last day of the crusade—the crowd doubled in size. We had one of the most unique healings I have ever witnessed: twin boys who were born deaf both received healing and could hear clearly.

I believe without doubt that prayer and fasting release the hand of God to work supernatural miracles. They allow God to do what He desires to do in situations and in ways we can never imagine or plan.

In fasting and praying, we do not change God's mind. Rather, we begin to understand God's mind. We have clearer insight on what God is doing and is going to do. We hear the heartbeat of God. We catch the vision of God for His kingdom to be established, souls to be saved, the sick to be healed, and the needy to be helped.

Our fasting and prayer do not change the will of heaven. Rather, our fasting and prayer make us participants in bringing heaven to this earth so that the prayer is fulfilled: "Thy kingdom come. Thy will be done in earth, as it is in heaven" (Matt. 6:10).

Our fasting and prayer do not conform God to our desires. Rather, our fasting and prayer conform us to God's desires for us!

ALWAYS A MATTER OF THE HEART

Just keeping a fast, in and of itself, produces no spiritual power. The purpose of the fast must be rooted firmly in what the Lord calls a person to do and be accompanied by prayer and a diligent seeking of God.

There are several occasions in the Bible in which people proclaimed a fast or taught others to fast, and what they did was not at all righteous.

The Lord spoke to the prophet Jeremiah, "Pray not for this people for their good. When they fast, I will not hear their cry; and when they offer burnt offering and an oblation, I will not accept them: but I will consume them by the sword, and by the famine, and by the pestilence." Why did the Lord refuse to honor the fasting of His people in this case? He revealed His reason to Jeremiah: "Thus have they loved to wander, they have not refrained their feet, therefore the LORD doth not accept them" (Jer. 14:10–12). The people were rebelliously pursuing false gods and going to "high places" to worship idols. Fasting meant nothing if the people did not have hearts to seek God.

Jezebel, one of the most wicked queens in history, proclaimed a fast in Israel. She wrote letters, saying, "Proclaim a fast, and set Naboth on high among the people: And set two men, sons of Belial, before him, to bear witness against him, saying, Thou didst blaspheme God and the king. And then carry him out, and stone him, that he may die" (1 Kings 21:9–10). The people did as she said. Jezebel was wrapping a rigged trial in the guise of a religious fast. She was attempting to give an air of worship to something that was totally opposite God's will—the murder of an innocent man—so she could claim his vineyard as a gift to her husband. God certainly did not honor that fast nor the activities people did during it.

Jesus taught that the practice of the Pharisees was wrong because their hearts were wrong: "They disfigure their faces, that they may appear unto men to fast" (Matt. 6:16). The outward keeping of a fast means nothing if the inward purpose for fasting is wrong.

The apostle Paul warned Timothy about false teachers who would teach false doctrines, including practices that might be related to fasts:

> Now the Spirit speaketh expressly, that in the latter times some shall depart from the faith, giving heed to seducing spirits, and doctrines of devils; speaking lies in hypocrisy; having their conscience seared with a hot iron; forbidding to marry, and commanding to abstain from meats, which God hath created to be received with thanksgiving of them which believe and know the truth. For every creature of God is good, and nothing to be refused, if it be received with thanksgiving: for it is sanctified by the word of God and prayer. (1 Timothy 4:1–5)

In this case, people were teaching that certain outward signs and practices were necessary for all believers as part of their salvation. Paul stood strongly against this. Fasting has nothing to do with a person's salvation. It is an accompaniment to prayer, which is part of a person's worship to God as that person seeks to grow in his or her relationship with the Lord.

Examine your life and your heart.

Seek God's will.

These are the foremost keys to experiencing God's presence and power as you fast and pray. They are also the keys to your *spiritual* growth.

4

TEN BASIC PRINCIPLES
OF PRAYER

Fasting turns a person away from a connection to the earth. Food and drink are the main connection we have when it comes to partaking of the earth's substance.

Prayer creates a connection with *heaven.*

Prayer is communicating with God—it is establishing a personal hotline into the throne room of the Lord. As you pray, I encourage you to refer frequently to the principles presented in this chapter.

PRINCIPLE #1: PRAY FREQUENTLY

The Bible tells us to pray "without ceasing" (1 Thess. 5:17). To pray without ceasing means that a person is continually in an attitude of prayer, so that an awareness of God and a need for God are continually at the forefront of a person's thinking. In other words, at any moment, a person might give voice to a request of God or to a statement of praise and thanksgiving. At no time are we ever commanded to *stop* praying for deliverance from evil or for God to make us whole.

PRINCIPLE #2: PRAY FOR ALL MANNER OF NEED

The Bible encourages us to pray for all things that we perceive we need. James 4:2 says, "Ye have not, because ye ask not." God encourages His people, "Ask of me, and I shall give thee the heathen for thine inheritance, and the uttermost parts of the earth for thy possession" (Ps. 2:8). The people of God throughout the Bible asked God for all manner of provision. They asked Him for protection and deliverance from their enemies. They asked Him for wisdom, courage, discernment, guidance, and insight into the Bible. They asked Him for healing of spirit, mind, and body. Jesus told His disciples that if they asked for anything in His name, He would do it (John 14:14).

PRINCIPLE #3: PRAY WITH FAITH

We are to pray with faith, believing that we will have what we request. James tells us that we are to "ask in faith, nothing wavering. For he that wavereth is like a wave of the sea driven with the wind and tossed. For let not that man think that he shall receive any thing of the Lord. A double minded man is unstable in all his ways" (James 1:6–8).

It is the prayer of *faith* that brings a person to wholeness—the sinner saved, the sick healed.

Jesus said:

> Have faith in God. For verily I say unto you, That whosoever shall say unto this mountain, Be thou removed, and be thou cast into the sea; and shall not doubt in his heart, but shall believe that those things which he saith shall come to pass; he shall have whatsoever he saith.
>
> Therefore I say unto you, What things soever ye de-

sire, when ye pray, believe that ye receive them, and ye shall have them. (Mark 11:22–24)

PRINCIPLE #4: PRAY WITH FOCUS

A time set apart for praying and fasting is a time for addressing very specific needs in our lives. The more we focus our prayers, the more we are aware of what we truly need and deeply desire. There's an old saying: "I didn't know what I thought until I heard myself speak." This is often true about our deepest spiritual longings. We often aren't aware of what we truly want God to do in our lives and in our relationships with other people until we give voice to our petitions.

My husband, Wally, once went on a forty-day fast with a specific focus for his prayers. At the time we needed another building for our church because we had outgrown our current one. Actually, the building we were in had been too small for us for about five years! At the time of Wally's fast, God opened up a shopping center to us—it was a beautiful, elegant facility with 260,000 square feet of space and we were able to purchase it for a quarter on the dollar of the asking price. That was a supernatural victory for us! We are still occupying that space today.

PRINCIPLE #5: PRAY BOLDLY

Hebrews 4:16 says, "Let us therefore come boldly unto the throne of grace, that we may obtain mercy, and find grace to help in time of need." Those who are in right standing with God—who have had a born-again experience—have total and free access to God at all times. We must be bold in asking the Lord to move in powerful ways in our lives and in the lives of other people throughout this earth.

PRINCIPLE #6: PRAY WITH FERVOR

A season of praying and fasting is a time for praying with intensity. At times you may need to cry out to God with a loud voice. People throughout the Bible certainly cried out to the Lord. Don't be embarrassed to raise your voice in prayer, especially if you are alone. A time of prayer and fasting is a time of emptying not only your physical self, but also all of your emotions and longings before the Lord. The Bible tells us, "The effectual fervent prayer of a righteous man availeth much" (James 5:16).

I describe *fervor* to others this way: "You'll have fire in your belly." The person who prays with fervor has such a strong motivation to pray and does so with such urgency, he feels almost as if his need to pray might consume him. In other words, he can't *not* pray. He feels driven to pray until God has met the need or until he feels assurance that God has heard and is responding to his prayer.

PRINCIPLE #7: PRAY IN ACCORD WITH THE WILL OF HEAVEN

Our prayers are to be in alignment with the will of heaven. This means to pray for those things that we believe God has promised to us and that are in full accordance with the way He has established heaven. Jesus taught His disciples to pray to their heavenly Father, "Thy kingdom come. Thy will be done in earth, as it is in heaven" (Matt. 6:10). We are to pray that things will begin to take shape in our lives and in the lives of others around us just as things take shape in heaven!

James 4:3 tells us the reason God does not answer some of our prayer requests the way we want: "Ye ask, and receive not, because ye ask amiss, that ye may consume it upon your lusts."

The will of heaven is that a person refrain from evil and become a giving, loving witness to the Lord Jesus Christ. God is not going to grant the petitions of a person who asks totally for himself in order to use a blessing to fulfill a lust of the flesh. (Galatians 5:19–21 is a passage that lists some of these lusts of the flesh that are against the Spirit of God.)

So how can we know that what we are praying is in line with God's will for us? Here are three ways:

1. Pray What the Bible Says

Pray what the Bible commands and what the Bible promises. God has given His Word to every person without any partiality to a person's race, age, culture, denominational background, social status, or even his maturity in the Lord. God does not prefer one person over another (Acts 10:34). What God promises in the Bible is for every person. That includes *you*!

Now in some cases, as we read the Bible we see that God has put conditions on some of His provisions and promises. God will not honor sin, for example, and He will not answer yes to a request that might cause a person to sin or create a situation in which sin is likely to occur. Neither will God reward those who are rebellious or who scoff at His Word. A number of promises in the Bible have conditions attached to them. We need to be very careful in saying, "God has not answered my prayer" when the truth is really that we haven't met the conditions for Him to answer our prayers.

On the other hand, God does not grant salvation on the basis of any kind of works on our part. The Bible makes this very clear: "For by grace are ye saved through faith; and that not of yourselves: it is the gift of God: not of works, lest any man should boast" (Eph. 2:8–9). God has placed no conditions in the Bible for salvation to be given to the person who truly believes that Jesus is the Son of God and that His death on the cross was the one complete, irreversible, and lasting sacrifice that ever needed to be made for sin. John 3:16 says, "For God so loved the world, that he gave his only begotten Son, that whosoever believeth in him should not perish, but have everlasting life." "Whosoever" means *whosoever* (see also Heb. 10:10).

Throughout the remaining chapters of this book, you are going to find Scriptures that present God's promises, commandments, and provisions related to various needs and conditions. Turn these verses from the Bible into prayer!

How can you do that? Let me give you a few examples.

- The Bible gives us these words of Jesus: "Come unto me, all ye that labour and are heavy laden, and I will give you rest. Take my yoke upon you, and learn of me; for I am meek and lowly in heart: and ye shall find rest unto your souls. For my yoke is easy, and my burden is light" (Matt. 11:28–30). How can we turn this into a prayer?

  "Heavenly Father, I am struggling right now. My burdens seem very heavy to me. I have no peace in my spirit, no rest in my heart. You said that if I came to You in this matter, You would give me the peace and resolution that I need. I am willing to line up my life with Your commandments and to study the Bible. I am willing to do things Your way. Just show me, Lord, what it is that You desire for me to do. Show me how You want me to live. I know that You alone have the answers that I need so I ask You, dear Lord, to show me Your answers for this situation I am facing."

Is that a prayer based upon the Bible and in total alignment with God's will? Absolutely!

- The Bible tells us, "He that hath ears to hear, let him hear" (Matt. 11:15). How can we turn that into a prayer?

"Heavenly Father, I want to hear whatever You desire to say to me. If there's anything clogging up my ability to hear Your voice or to understand what You are trying to say to me as I read the Bible, which is Your Word to me, then please free up my ability to hear and to understand. I want to hear You so I can obey You. Help me to discern what it is You desire, and then give me the courage to walk out Your desire in my daily life."

Is that a prayer based upon the Bible and in total alignment with God's will? Absolutely!

- The Bible gives us these words of Jesus: "Seek ye first the kingdom of God, and his righteousness; and all these things shall be added unto you" (Matt. 6:33). How can we turn that into a prayer?

  "Heavenly Father, I know that the key to having everything I need is to seek You first and to desire to become a person who is in right standing with You. Show me, Lord, how to seek first the kingdom of God. Show me what it is that You consider to be righteousness. Show me how to make decisions that are in line with Your desires. Show me what it takes to walk in obedience and in faith before You. I want to trust You and to obey You. Show me, Lord, how to trust, and then I ask You to help me to obey."

Is that a prayer based upon the Bible and in total alignment with God's will? Yes, indeed!

2. Pray to Know God's Will

If you have read God's Word and still have questions about the specific will of God in your situation, ask the Lord to reveal His will to you. Ask for God's wisdom on the matter. James 1:5 tells us, "If any of you lack wisdom, let him ask of God, that giveth to all men liberally, and upbraideth not; and it shall be given him." God desires to pour out His wisdom on those who genuinely seek to have it—He never ridicules or chides us for asking. He delights in giving His wisdom to us in abundance.

The Lord desires to reveal to you everything you need to know to live a godly, Christ-centered life on this earth. He desires to reveal to you everything you need to know to live an abundant life—and to experience all the blessings God has for you in your spirit, mind, body, relationships, and finances. He desires to reveal to you how to win others to Christ and how to do the things that bring the greatest fulfillment, joy, and sense of purpose every hour of every day.

Ask the Lord to do what He desires to do in you, through you, and all around you. He will answer your prayer!

3. Pray with a Yielding Spirit

The third way we can pray according to God's will is to yield whatever we request to the Lord just as Jesus did. In the Garden of Gethsemane, Jesus prayed to His Father: "Father, if thou be willing, remove this cup from me: nevertheless not my will, but thine, be done" (Luke 22:42). There is great wisdom in saying to the Lord about anything we ask of Him, "Father, this is my desire, my need as I see it, but I recognize that You see all things. You alone know if this is Your highest and best for me. I want Your highest and best in all things, so if my request is not in keeping with Your will, I ask for Your will to be done, not mine."

PRINCIPLE #8: PRAY WITH FRIENDS

Participating in a time of fasting and prayer with other people brings tremendous benefit. Meet regularly with others who will pray both *with* you and *for* you. In turn, this is an opportunity for you to give prayers to others as a seed of your faith so that God might multiply your prayers back to you in the form of the answers and solutions you need most. Every prayer has within it the seed of a future miracle!

Jesus said, "If two of you shall agree on earth as touching any thing that they shall ask, it shall be done for them of my Father which is in heaven. For where two or three are gathered together in my name, there am I in the midst of them" (Matt. 18:19–20). Come to a point of agreement with others about what you truly know to be the will of heaven in a particular situation.

PRINCIPLE #9: PRAY AS THE SPIRIT LEADS

Pray always as the Spirit leads you. Very often the Spirit leads us in prayer once we have started praying. Even as you are in the middle of a prayer, ask the Holy Spirit to guide your thoughts and words. Ask Him to reveal to you what He desires to hear from you in the form of praise and thanksgiving. Ask Him to reveal to you what He desires for you to pray, not only for yourself but for others.

PRINCIPLE #10: PRAY WITH COMPASSION

One of the foremost ways you can express compassion to another person is to touch that person as you pray.

If you are praying and agreeing with another person who is standing or sitting close to you, I recommend that you reach out to one another and hold hands or put your arms on each other's shoulders. There is tremendous benefit in touching as a means of agreeing and of sharing a time of prayer together.

The Bible teaches us to lay hands on the sick. We read in

James 5:14–15: "Is any sick among you? Let him call for the elders of the church; and let them pray over him, anointing him with oil in the name of the Lord; and the prayer of faith shall save the sick, and the Lord shall raise him up; and if he have committed sins, they shall be forgiven him." To anoint a person with oil meant to touch that person—it meant to place one's hands on a person.

You are always wise to ask if a person is comfortable with your touching him or her as you pray. In the vast majority of cases, people will welcome your touch and your prayers. People are starving today for genuine expressions of godly love.

If you are interceding for a person, I encourage you to put your hand over your own heart as you pray. Remind yourself in this expression of love that you desire for the other person to experience the fullness of God's love in his or her life.

5

A TWENTY-ONE-DAY FAST FOR A BREAKTHROUGH IN HABITS

Much of the healing and wholeness that God desires for us is related to habits, and certainly issues related to our physical health and material provision are often rooted in our habits.

- Our physical healing and health are linked to habits we have related to eating, exercising, and sleeping.
- Our emotional healing and health are linked to habits we have in the way we relate to other people and to the way we think about ourselves and others.
- Our spiritual healing and health are linked to habits—often called *spiritual disciplines*—that are important to our relationship with God. These include habits such as praying and fasting, but also reading and studying the Bible, attending and serving others in a church, and being involved in various ministries that reach out to people in need.

Many times even our relationships with family members and friends are impacted by the habits we have developed when it comes to communication, doing the chores required for keeping a home, and maintaining a daily or weekly schedule.

DEVELOPING HABITS FOR WHOLENESS

One of the things we know about habits is that we can make them. We can learn them, decide to do them, break bad ones, and establish new ones. Habits are subject to change. In many cases, a time of fasting and prayer leads a person to recognize the changes he needs to make in his habits.

Another thing we know about habits is that they provide a framework for our lives. What we do on any given day reveals our priorities. What we continue to keep as habits ultimately define our character, and our character determines our reputations and our impact on this world. For example, if a person eats right, prays, exercises, and reads God's Word every day, he has obviously made spiritual and physical health top priorities. These daily habits show that the person is disciplined and very likely has a strong purpose for living. Over time, the person will be renewed in his mind by the reading of God's Word. He will be healthier in his body, and he will draw closer to the Lord.

People who see this person's life will very likely see a person who has vitality, energy, commitment, steadfastness, and spiritual maturity. This person is likely to have greater health as he ages, and he will have more energy for doing God's work for more years. None of this can be predicted with certainty, of course, but daily habits are a strong indicator of trends in a person's life, and trends reap fairly predictable consequences over time.

We may not like to confront them, but scientific research bears out these facts:

- The person who smokes cigarettes *every day over decades* is much more likely to have heart disease and cancer.
- The person who eats the wrong foods in the wrong quantities *every day over decades* is much more likely to have a wide variety of serious health problems as the years go by.

- The person who stays out in the sun without sunscreen protection for long periods of time *every day over decades* is likely to have damaged skin and is more likely to have skin cancer.

Countless trends such as these manifest themselves over time. Most of them go back to daily habits, or frequent use.

What is true in the negative is also true in the positive. The person who develops good habits reaps good results. The Bible, of course, presents this truth clearly: "Be not deceived; God is not mocked: for whatsoever a man soweth, that shall he also reap. . . . And let us not be weary in well doing: for in due season we shall reap, if we faint not" (Gal. 6:7, 9).

Developing New Habits

Research through the years has confirmed an interesting fact about habits: it takes about twenty-one days to change one, quit one, or adopt one. Nobody seems to know exactly why this time period seems linked to learning new behaviors, but there is strong evidence that a three-week period is what it takes to rewire a person's behavior in a conscious way.

I do not think it's any accident that the number twenty-one has been equated with holy perfection. Throughout the Bible, three is the number associated with the Holy Trinity and seven is the number linked to fulfillment, completion, wholeness, or perfection. Thus, 3 x 7 = 21 . . . a number representing the power of God multiplying into our lives what God perceives we need for wholeness or perfection.

Bad Habits vs. Evil Behaviors

We need to recognize that there's a difference between bad habits and evil habits. Evil habits have an element of rebellion and sin in them. They involve willful disobedience against the commands of God at some point in the formation of the habit.

For example, a person who is obsessed with the idea of having an adulterous affair generally knows that the idea is wrong—but then becomes so caught up in the idea that he can't seem to break the habitual pattern of thinking. As another example, a person who finds herself in a terribly abusive work-related relationship may very well recognize early on that something is wrong with the relationship, but over time, the patterns or habit of the abuse has become so engrained that the person no longer sees that release from the relationship is possible.

Bad habits more commonly have an element of neglect to them. People often neglect to do what is good, or they put off doing what they know they should do. In some cases, they may never have known that a certain habit could lead to great harm.

When personal habits are related to evil, they nearly always are habits in the way a person thinks or believes. An obsession, for example, is a habitual way of returning again and again to the same topic, the same issue, the same person, the same idea. In many addictions, a person has adopted a lie in what he believes about himself and his inability to cope with life unless he partakes of a particular substance. Habits that are rooted in lies have an element of evil to them.

Confronting Your Personal Habits

Countless things might be considered daily habits. I've listed more than thirty activities or behaviors here to give you an idea about the variety and scope of daily habits:

1. Spending time in prayer.
2. Spending time reading the Bible.
3. Listening to the news.
4. Taking a bath or shower.
5. Brushing your hair.
6. Brushing and flossing your teeth.

7. Keeping a personal hygiene or makeup ritual.
8. Checking the mail and e-mail.
9. Working.
10. Exercising—various types for various results.
11. Eating the right foods in the right amounts.
12. Drinking sufficient water.
13. Sitting quietly and listening for the Lord to speak to your heart.
14. Answering and returning phone calls.
15. Taking medications.
16. Attending to the special needs of a particular family member, perhaps a child or elderly parent.
17. Taking vitamins and food supplements.
18. Working on a special project.
19. Doing the crossword puzzle in the newspaper.
20. Writing in a personal diary or journal.
21. Taking care of family pets.
22. Taking the children to school and picking them up.
23. Helping children with homework.
24. Making a "priority of the day" list of things to accomplish.
25. Preparing family meals.
26. Running errands.
27. Doing various household chores.
28. Doing various yard-related chores.
29. Doing something for sheer fun.
30. Giving someone a big hug.
31. Putting change from a purse or pocket into a savings jar.
32. Talking to family members or friends about the day's activities.
33. Studying or reading for pleasure or for work, as part of preparing for a Bible study, or for some other reason.
34. Telling someone that you love him or her.
35. Setting an alarm clock for the next day.
36. Sleeping—and perhaps taking a power nap.

Virtually all of these habits are good ones—ones that we develop and keep one day at a time. We can develop or change any of these habits in a three-week time period.

As you go into a time of fasting and praying, ask the Lord what new habits He desires for you to adopt. Ask Him which habits He desires for you to quit or alter. Expect God to lead you to change something! Don't go into a time of fasting and prayer assuming that the status quo of your daily habits is going to remain the same as you come out of this season of seeking God.

Recognizing Habits in Your Family

The habits that exist in families tend to be clustered in four categories:

1. *Habits in the way people relate to one another.* Some of these habits have to do with communication, others with manners.
2. *Habits in the schedules the family keeps.* Having a family routine is a form of habit. Praying together by a bedside each night, reading the Bible together as a family over breakfast, and going to church and Sunday school together as a family each week are among the habits that are embedded in a family schedule.
3. *Habits in the way people conduct certain rituals and celebrations.* Every family seems to have its own set of habits when it comes to the way it marks holidays, birthdays, and important events such as the dedication of a baby, a wedding, or a funeral.
4. *Habits in the way the family does things.* For example, how the parents divide the workload into individual chores, reward good behavior, discipline bad behavior, plan and make decisions about matters such as family vacation, and choose to attend or not attend certain functions as a family.

As you go into a time of fasting and praying for your family, ask the Lord if He is pleased with the way you relate to each member in your family—if He would like for you to add something to your family schedule or take something out of it . . . if He is pleased with the way you celebrate or mark various events . . . if He desires for you to change the way you divide responsibility, discipline or reward your children, make decisions and plans, or do things together as a family.

Recognize that you cannot change a family habit by yourself. You will need the cooperation of other family members. If the Lord leads you to make a change in the habits of your family, ask Him also to show you how to approach your family and to gain their cooperation in making the change He desires.

BEGINNING THE YEAR WITH A TWENTY-ONE-DAY FAST

I've mentioned that for years, the people in our church—Orchard Road Christian Center in Greenwood Village, Colorado—have started each year with a twenty-one-day period for prayer and fasting. This is a time when the people come together to encourage one another and to pray in a concerted way for changes they desire to see in their lives. There's a feeling of high expectancy! People see this time as a new beginning, a time of breakthrough, a time of pushing forward toward excellence, a time of seeing miracles when it comes to weight loss, finances, healing, and deliverance for families and addictions.

As a very practical consideration, I should tell you that we do not start this churchwide time of fasting and praying on January 1. This season of fasting and praying is far more serious than the making of a New Year's resolution. What we have discovered through the years is that many people who make New Year's resolutions have a very difficult time keeping them the first few days of the year! There are simply too many parties, too many activities, too much travel, and too many pressures during the first few days of January. You may want to begin your twenty-one-day fast the Monday after New Year's Day.

Here are four things that we encourage people to do during this first-of-the-year fast:

1. Have a Focus or Theme for Each Day

Jesus gave an illustration about how we are to ask the Lord for things in our lives. He said, "Which of you shall have a friend, and shall go unto him at midnight, and say unto him, Friend, lend me three loaves?" (Luke 11:5). Jesus did not say, "Lend me some bread." He very specifically had this man requesting three loaves! God wants us to be specific in voicing to Him our needs. No need is too small or too great, but a need can be so general that we don't have a real intensity of focus as we pray. Ultimately, if our prayers are general, we often don't know when we have received answers to them.

Your focus each day is not only during your prayer times, but it is also the focus of your meditation or contemplation throughout the day. Force your mind to return to the focus of each day as you drive to and from work, wait for appointments, or run errands. Ask the Lord to reveal new insights to you that are associated with the focus of the day.

I have listed twenty-one areas for focus later in the chapter, but you may come up with a list of your own. Sometimes a particular habit or purpose for our fasting can be broken down into very specific pieces that need to be addressed in concerted prayer. Ask the Lord how He desires for you to organize your own season of fasting and praying.

2. Have a Bible Verse as Part of Your Daily Theme or Focus

I encourage you to memorize the Bible verse that is associated with the theme of each day in a twenty-one-day fast. If your entire family is fasting, speak this verse aloud to one another during the day. Repeated speaking of the verse is the best way to memorize. You probably will find that if you read aloud a verse seven to ten times during a day, you will have memorized it by the time you go to bed.

I have listed Bible verses later in the chapter that accompany the various themes for each day in a twenty-one-day fast. If you have developed your own list of daily themes, be sure to find a verse to go with each one.

3. Write Down a Very Specific Prayer for Each Day

This can be a few words or a longer statement of prayer. You might list a particular person's name or a particular attitude associated with the day's focus. Voice the prayer aloud to the Lord.

4. Reflect upon Each Day

Take a few minutes at the end of each day to reflect upon what you may have gained as an insight into God's Word, what the Lord may have spoken to your heart, a prayer someone may have prayed for you, or a word of encouragement that someone may have spoken to you related to your purpose in fasting. You will be greatly blessed as you read back over these statements at the end of your season of fasting and prayer, and you will be blessed repeatedly as you read back over these statements in the weeks, months, or years ahead.

In the back of this book, you will find an Appendix titled "Daily Journal for a Twenty-One-Day Season of Fasting and Praying." This is a page you may duplicate for your use. Feel free to use the theme statements and verses I'll list next in any way that you desire.

You and you alone know the greater purpose you have for entering a season of fasting and praying. If you are fasting and praying for the adjustment of your habits, you alone know the habits you are seeking to adopt or change. For virtually any change of habit, however, the areas of focus listed below can apply.

FOCUS THEMES AND SCRIPTURE VERSES
FOR TWENTY-ONE DAYS

DAY	FOCUS OR THEME

---

1   The power of God is working in my life.
        Verse: 2 Peter 1:3
        "According as his divine power hath given unto us all things that pertain unto life and godliness, through the knowledge of him that hath called us to glory and virtue."

2   I will believe God for increase.
        Verse: Psalm 115:14–16
        "The LORD shall increase you more and more, you and your children. Ye are blessed of the LORD which made heaven and earth. The heaven, even the heavens, are the LORD's: but the earth hath he given to the children of men."

3   I will believe God for greater strength.
        Verse: Nehemiah 8:10
        "Then he said unto them, Go your way, eat the fat, and drink the sweet, and send portions unto them for whom nothing is prepared: for this day is holy unto our Lord: neither be ye sorry; for the joy of the LORD is your strength."

4   God is meeting *all* of my needs.
        Verse: Psalm 34:10
        "The young lions do lack, and suffer hunger: but they that seek the LORD shall not want any good thing."

5   I will walk in the love of God and express God's love to others.

Verse: 1 John 2:15

"Love not the world, neither the things that are in the world. If any man love the world, the love of the Father is not in him."

6   I will persevere until I see total victory—I will settle for nothing less.

Verse: Isaiah 54:17

"No weapon that is formed against thee shall prosper; and every tongue that shall rise against thee in judgment thou shalt condemn. This is the heritage of the servants of the LORD, and their righteousness is of me, saith the LORD."

7   I will trust God's Word to give me direction and guidance.

Verse: Proverbs 6:22

"When thou goest, it shall lead thee; when thou sleepest, it shall keep thee; and when thou wakest, it shall talk with thee."

8   I am believing for good things to happen to and in my family.

Verse: Psalm 112:1–3

"Praise ye the LORD. Blessed is the man that feareth the LORD, that delighteth greatly in his commandments. His seed shall be mighty upon earth: the generation of the upright shall be blessed. Wealth and riches shall be in his house: and his righteousness endureth for ever."

9   I will walk in God's promises.

Verse: 2 Peter 1:4

"Whereby are given unto us exceeding great and precious promises: that by these ye might be partakes of the divine nature, having escaped the corruption that is in the world through lust."

10   I will seek God's will until I know it and then declare God's will in every situation of my life.
Verse: Romans 8:27
"And he that searcheth the hearts knoweth what is the mind of the Spirit, because he maketh intercession for the saints according to the will of God."

11   I will seek to live by God's principles for divine health.
Verse: Jeremiah 17:14
"Heal me, O LORD, and I shall be healed; save me, and I shall be saved: for thou art my praise."

12   I will not worry—I will trust that God is in control of all things and He will take care of me!
Verse: 1 Peter 5:7
"Casting all your care upon him; for he careth for you."

13   God will not withhold any good thing from my life.
Verse: Psalm 84:11
"For the LORD God is a sun and shield: the LORD will give grace and glory: no good thing will he withhold from them that walk uprightly."

14   I will speak words of peace in every problem situation.
Verse: Isaiah 26:3
"Thou wilt keep him in perfect peace, whose mind is stayed on thee: because he trusteth in thee."

15   I will voice my heart's desires to the Lord and believe that God is in the process of giving me my heart's desires.
Verse: Psalm 37:4
"Delight thyself also in the LORD; and he will give thee the desires of thine heart."

16   I will make knowing God's will the highest priority of my life.

Verse: Matthew 7:21

"Not everyone who says to me, 'Lord, Lord,' will enter the kingdom of heaven, but only he who does the will of my Father who is in heaven." (NIV)

17   I believe God is breaking all generational curses in my life and the lives of my family members.

Verse: Romans 12:1–2

"Therefore, I urge you, brothers, in view of God's mercy, to offer your bodies as living sacrifices, holy and pleasing to God—this is your spiritual act of worship. Do not conform any longer to the pattern of this world, but be transformed by the renewing of your mind. Then you will be able to test and approve what God's will is—his good, pleasing and perfect will." (NIV)

18   I am special and beloved in God's eyes.

Verse: Zechariah 2:8

"For thus saith the LORD of hosts; After the glory hath he sent me unto the nations which spoiled you: for he that toucheth you toucheth the apple of his eye."

19   I will walk in God's mercy and rejoice.

Verse: Psalm 13:5

"I have trusted in thy mercy; my heart shall rejoice in thy salvation."

20   I will be bold for God!

Verse: Proverbs 28:1

"The wicked flee when no man pursueth: but the righteous are bold as a lion."

21   I am trusting God for the salvation of all my loved ones.

Verse: Isaiah 8:18

"Behold, I and the children whom the LORD hath given me are for signs and for wonders in Israel from the LORD of hosts, which dwelleth in mount Zion."

A CHANGE IN HABITS CAN BRING BREAKTHROUGH!

What we have discovered through the years is that a change in habits can bring genuine and lasting breakthroughs in a person's life. What is established in a season of fasting and prayer has a good likelihood of lasting a lifetime. Many people go into a twenty-one-day fast in order to:

- Establish or extend a regular time each day spent in reading the Bible and praying.
- Lose weight or jump-start a weight-loss program that results in new thinking patterns and eating habits.
- Extend or adopt a new exercise routine—or begin exercising after years of not exercising.
- Stop smoking or drinking alcohol.
- See family members reconciled or problems resolved.
- Begin a new financial plan, one that includes tithing, investing, becoming free of debt, and living within a balanced budget.
- Start a new habit of reading and studying to grow in knowledge, understanding, and wisdom.
- Break a negative cycle of fear, doubt, or worry.
- Become free of old hatreds, prejudices, and bitter attitudes.

A twenty-one-day fast puts a person on the right track. It sets a pattern. It establishes a new rhythm of life. It turns one's thinking around. It creates a new hunger for what is good and right in God's eyes. As you read through the remaining chapters of this book, look for ways in which you might take on new habits to see God's purposes fully accomplished in your life.

6

CHOOSING THE FAST THAT'S RIGHT FOR YOU

If you are going to fast and pray, you need the Spirit to lead you. This is true no matter what type of fast you undertake. The Bible tells us, "Then was Jesus led up of the spirit into the wilderness" (Matt. 4:1).

As the Holy Spirit leads you into a time of fasting, recognize that you must obey a true call to fast. Don't delay. Don't wait for church leaders to call a time of fasting and praying. Don't wait for the first of the year, or any other start time that seems appropriate to your own schedule or calendar. Prepare and begin immediately to obey God's call to fast.

Ask God for four things:

1. Ask the Lord to confirm His call to fast and pray. The Holy Spirit will not prompt you to do something without confirming His will for you in the Scriptures or through the preaching and teaching of godly leaders. Look and listen closely for how the Spirit leads. (This book may be God's confirming word to you!)

2. Ask the Lord to reveal to you the specific breakthrough you need in your life. You need to know the core purpose for

praying and fasting so you might arm yourself spiritually with Scriptures as you pray God's will into your life and the lives of your loved ones.

3. Ask the Lord to reveal to you the things you should expect as you pray and fast. Talk to the Lord about the desires He has for you. You need to have a very clear goal and direction about what it is that you are seeking God to do in your life, through your life, and in circumstances, situations, relationships, or the lives of your loved ones.

4. Ask the Lord to show you which fast is right for you.

OBEDIENCE IS REQUIRED!

This matter of obedience in praying and fasting is extremely important. We have a dramatic example in the Bible of a fast that people did not keep. The results were disastrous. The Word of God came to the prophet Jeremiah about a very specific fast God wanted His people to undertake. It was for a specific reason, with the potential for a great reward if the people would keep it.

Let me give you a little background on this event. Jehoiakim, the king of Judah, had imprisoned Jeremiah. The Lord spoke to Jeremiah in his confinement and said,

> Take a scroll of a book and write on it all the words that I have spoken to you against Israel, against Judah, and against all the nations, from the day I spoke to you, from the days of Josiah even to this day. It may be that the house of Judah will hear all the adversities which I purpose to bring upon them, that everyone may turn from his evil way, that I may forgive their iniquity and their sin. (Jeremiah 36:2–3 NKJV)

God made it very clear that His desire was for the people to hear the Word of God as they fasted and to repent in prayer. If they did so, God would keep King Nebuchadnezzar from attacking the people and wiping them out.

Jeremiah called his scribe and assistant, Baruch, to write down the words of the Lord on a scroll as Jeremiah dictated them. Then Jeremiah sent Baruch with the scroll to the house of the Lord with the instruction to read it on the day of fasting. Baruch did as he was told.

We read: "And it came to pass in the fifth year of Jehoiakim the son of Josiah, king of Judah, in the ninth month, that they proclaimed a fast before the LORD to all the people in Jerusalem, and to all the people that came from the cities of Judah to Jerusalem" (Jer. 36:9 NKJV).

Baruch read the book of Jeremiah's words in the chamber of Gemariah the son of Shaphan the scribe, "in the hearing of all the people." When Gemariah's son Michaiah heard the words, he went down to the king's house into the scribe's chamber. There he found all the princes of Judah. Michaiah declared to them all the words Baruch had read to the people. The princes sent for Baruch and demanded that he read the words directly to them. Baruch did so. The princes were so fearful of what the king's reaction might be that they told Baruch to "go and hide" (Jer. 36:10, 19 NKJV). The scroll was stored in the official scribe chambers and in due course, a man named Jehudi read the scroll to the king.

The Bible tells us that Jehudi read the word of the Lord as given to Jeremiah while the king was sitting in his winter palace with a fire burning in his hearth. The princes of Judah were also in the room. After Jehudi had read three or four columns of the word, the king took the scroll into his own hands, cut it up with a knife, and cast it into the fire!

The king refused to hear or heed the word of the Lord and as a result, the princes of Judah refused to hear or heed it. In turn, the people followed the example of their leaders. Israel did not complete the fast by repenting in prayer. And in the end, Nebuchadnezzar did conquer the people, the king was punished severely and died, and the people of Judah were swept into captivity by the Babylonians.

If God calls you to fast . . . obey Him!

A LONG OR SHORT FAST?

There is no automatic benefit linked to the length of time you fast. What matters before the Lord is that you obey His commands and get your heart in line with His desires for you.

Years ago, shortly after my husband, Wally, began to serve the Lord, he had a friend in a mental hospital about whom he was very concerned. Wally had never been taught about fasting but as he prayed for his friend, the Lord spoke to him out of the Scriptures, saying, "Howbeit this kind goeth not out but by prayer and fasting" (Matt. 17:21). Wally didn't know how long to fast, so he fasted one meal and prayed during that mealtime. Even after Wally's short time of fasting and praying, the man was released from the hospital!

At the other end of the spectrum, Wally has also spent forty days fasting and praying on two occasions in his life.

Long or short is not the critical factor in a fast. It's as the Lord leads!

Fasts in the Bible

In all, there are references to at least twenty-five specific individuals or groups of people who fasted. I have listed them below in order as each person or group first appears in the Bible. As you look through this list, note that the list includes men and women. It includes people in the Old Testament and New Testament. In some cases, the person or group fasted on more than one occasion, and in some cases, they fasted for different lengths of time on dif-

ferent occasions. In more than a third of these references, we do
not know how long the personal or group fast lasted.

FASTS IN THE BIBLE

PERSON/GROUP FASTING	LENGTH OF FAST	BIBLE REFERENCE
1. Joshua	forty days	Exod. 24:13–18, 32:15–17
2. Moses	forty days	Deut. 9:9, 18, 25–29, 10:10
3. Israel	one day	Judg. 20:26–35
	seven days	1 Sam. 31:13
4. David	one day	2 Sam. 1:12, 3:35
	seven days	2 Sam. 12:16–23
	unknown	Ps. 35:13, 69:10, 109:24
5. Elijah	forty days	1 Kings 19:7–18
6. Ahab	unknown	1 Kings 21:27–29
7. Judah	unknown	2 Chron. 20:1–25
		Ezra 8:21–23
	one day	Neh. 9:1–4; Jer. 36:6
8. Ezra	unknown	Ezra 10:6–17
9. Nehemiah	unknown	Neh. 1:4–2:10
10. Jews	unknown	Esther 4:1–3, 9:1–3
11. Esther	three days	Esther 4:13–16, 5:1, 9:3
12. Mordecai	three days	Esther 4:13–16, 5:1, 9
13. Darius	one night	Dan. 6:18–24
14. Daniel	one day	Dan. 9:3, 20–27
	twenty-one days	Dan. 10:3–13
15. People of Nineveh	unknown	Jonah 3
16. Jesus	forty days	Matt. 4:1–11

PERSON/GROUP FASTING	LENGTH OF FAST	BIBLE REFERENCE
17. John's disciples	unknown	Matt. 9:14–15
18. Many people	three days	Matt. 15:32–39
19. Anna	unknown	Luke 2:37
20. Pharisee	one day	Luke 18:9–14
21. Church at Antioch	unknown	Acts 13:1–5
22. Paul	three days	Acts 9:9, 17
	unknown	Acts 27:9–11; 2 Cor. 6:5, 11:27
23. Cornelius	unknown	Acts 10
24. Many churches	unknown	Acts 14:23
25. Paul and 276 men	fourteen days	Acts 27:33–34

WHAT SHOULD WE GIVE UP?

The Bible story of Hannah begins with a feast. Hannah and her husband, Elkanah, had gone with Elkanah's entire family to make an annual trip to Shiloh, the place where the ark of the covenant was located at that time. This was a worship trip—a time of sacrifice to the Lord and also a time of feasting.

Hannah, who was "sore in spirit," got up from the feasting table and went to the entrance of the tabernacle, which was as far as she was allowed to go. There, Hannah wept and prayed before the Lord. When Eli, the high priest, found her there he saw her praying and crying, but only her lips were moving—she wasn't making any sounds. He accused her of being drunk. Hannah replied, "No, my lord, I am a woman of a sorrowful spirit: I have drunk neither wine nor strong drink, but have poured out my soul before the LORD" (1 Sam. 1:15).

We have no mention that Hannah fasted from food, but she did fast from fermented beverages, something that was common to feasts at that time.

Through the years, a number of people have told me that they have fasted from various food groups. In our first-of-the-year, twenty-one-day seasons of praying and fasting, people give up a variety of things. Some do a strict water-only fast. Some include natural, no-sugar-added fruit juices. Some do a pleasant-meat fast. The Bible actually gives mention to three specialized fasts:

1. *No cereals or grains.* This fast is actually part of the Feast of Firstfruits. During this time, God commanded the Israelites: "Ye shall eat neither bread, nor parched corn, nor green ears, until the selfsame day that ye have brought an offering unto your God" (Lev. 23:14).

2. *No grape products.* Part of the Nazarite vow, which was most notably kept by the judge Samson all of his life, was this command of the Lord: "He shall separate himself from wine and strong drink, and shall drink no vinegar of wine, or vinegar of strong drink, neither shall he drink any liquor of grapes, nor eat moist grapes, or dried" (Num. 6:3).

3. *No meat.* The fast that Daniel and his friends kept in Babylon was a vegetarian fast. Daniel and his friends had been taken into captivity and the king of Babylon, Nebuchadnezzar, had ordered that they be fed daily a provision of the king's meat, most of which was either not on the approved list of foods or was not prepared in an acceptable way according to the Jewish dietary laws in the Old Testament. Daniel said to the authorities over him,

> Prove thy servants, I beseech thee, ten days; and let them give us pulse to eat, and water to drink. ["Pulse" is an Old English word for vegetables!] Then let our countenances

be looked upon before thee, and the countenance of the children that eat of the portion of the king's meat: and as thou seest, deal with thy servants. So he consented to them in this matter, and proved them ten days. And at the end of ten days their countenances appeared fair and fatter in flesh than all the children which did eat the portion of the king's meat. Thus Melzar took away the portion of their meat, and the wine that they should drink; and gave them pulse. (Daniel 1:12–16)

In the New Testament, the apostle Paul encouraged believers to abstain from meats and beverages that had been offered to idols. The custom in many Roman cities was for major sacrifices to be made daily and then for the bulk of the sacrificed foods to be sold in an open marketplace. Paul made it very clear that there was nothing wrong in God's eyes with this meat—the idols were not real, and therefore the sacrifice made to them was a moot point.

However, Paul said, some of your Christian brothers are offended at the idea of eating meat that had been offered to an idol. They found it to be a distraction to their own prayers and worship of God. Paul admonished: don't do what causes an offense to a fellow believer. In other words, don't do anything that might hinder the prayers and worship of other people. He wrote to the Corinthians, "If meat make my brother to offend, I will eat no flesh while the world standeth, lest I make my brother to offend" (1 Cor. 8:13; see also Rom. 14:20–21).

In most cases, fasting will be an abstaining from all food. (A total fast—which is a fast that also requires abstinence from water—is not recommended for longer than three days. Before commencing a fast, you should assess your health and consider visiting a health professional.)

Again, it is not a matter of what you eat or don't eat. It's a matter of how the Lord leads you to fast.

ALONE OR WITH OTHERS?

Some people fast on an individual basis. Others fast as part of a group that is fasting and praying—for church-related as well as individual purposes.

The Bible includes several examples of the Israelites coming together as a group to fast and worship God. For example, the people fasted at Mizpeh as a sign of their repentance for sins against the Lord (1 Sam. 7:6). Saul's army was ordered to fast before a battle (1 Sam. 14:24). After the deaths of Saul and Jonathan in battle, the people of Jabesh-gilead fasted for seven days, and when the "mighty men" of David heard about the death of Saul and his son, they also mourned, wept, and fasted (1 Chron. 10:10–12; 2 Sam. 1:12). Both King Jehoshaphat and King Jehoiakim called the nation to fast (2 Chron. 20:3–4; Jer. 36:9–10).

One of the most interesting group fasts in the Bible is the one the king of Nineveh ordered. God had sent the prophet Jonah to proclaim God's anger against them. The Bible says:

> So the people of Nineveh believed God, and proclaimed a fast, and put on sackcloth, from the greatest of them even to the least of them. For word came unto the king of Nineveh, and he arose from his throne, and he laid his robe from him, and covered him with sackcloth, and sat in ashes. And he caused it to be proclaimed and published through Nineveh by the decree of the king and his nobles, saying, Let neither man nor beast, herd nor flock, taste anything: let them not feed, nor drink water: But let man and beast be covered with sackcloth, and cry mightily unto God: yea, let them turn every one from his evil way, and from the violence that is in their hands. (Jonah 3:5–8)

The people of Nineveh were not Jews! Nineveh was the capital of the Assyrian empire. The Ninevites were Assyrians, the archenemies of the Jews. The Assyrians had invaded Israel on several occasions, always with much bloodshed and oppression. Nevertheless, God cared enough about these people to send a prophet to them. When the Ninevites heard Jonah cry out the word of the Lord, they believed God. Their believing led them to proclaim a fast. The fast was not instead of believing God—in other words, they didn't cling to their old ways and put on an exterior trapping of a fast in order to try to appear acceptable to God. From the king down to the lowliest servant, they covered themselves with sackcloth and ashes as a sign of their genuine belief that God had spoken to them a harsh word of warning and rebuke. Isn't it amazing that the Ninevites caused even their animals to fast? They were sincere!

Notice what the king commanded his people to do: "Let them turn every one from his evil way, and from the violence that is in their hands" (Jon. 3:8). Their "evil way" refers to their way of thinking, believing, and feeling. The king ordered the Ninevites to give up their hatred of the Jews and to change their minds and hearts about the God of Israel. They were to give up all desires for revenge and conquest. "The violence that is in their hands" refers to behavior—to doing something, to actions that are violent. The king was ordering his people to put down their weapons of war.

This was a fast that was internal to the hearts of the Ninevites, not just an outward show. And what was the result? God spared the city. The Bible tells us that God "saw their works, that they turned from their evil way"—He saw both what they did in their behavior and in their hearts—and God did not wipe out the city (Jon. 3:9).

We should also recognize that God was watching the heart of Jonah as well as the hearts of the Ninevites. The Lord saw unforgiveness in the heart of Jonah and He spoke very harsh words to Jonah because the prophet refused to accept the Lord's forgiveness of the Assyrians.

Jonah had rebelled against going to Nineveh in the first place. The Assyrians were the last people he wanted to see repent. They were terribly cruel and violent, and Jonah wanted God to destroy them. Jonah ran away, but eventually—by way of a great fish that God prepared for the rebellious prophet—Jonah arrived in the city with a very simple message: "Repent!" To his surprise, the Assyrians did. Jonah sat under a vine and cried because God didn't kill this enemy of Israel.

If anybody needed to fast, it was Jonah! He should have gone into a time of fasting and prayer to prepare himself as God's messenger to Nineveh, but he didn't. Why do I say that? Because a time of fasting and prayer was definitely what God had in mind for this resistant prophet who did *not* want to obey the word of the Lord. It certainly was no accident that the Lord put Jonah into a situation in which he was forced to fast and eventually to pray.

The Bible tells us that Jonah was in the belly of the great fish for three days and nights. While in the belly of that fish, Jonah was on a God-imposed fast! There was nothing he wanted to eat, perhaps nothing he could eat, in the belly of that great fish. Jonah 2:1 tells us, "Then Jonah prayed unto the LORD his God out of the fish's belly." Jonah finally came to grips with God's call and cried out to the Lord for mercy. Jonah prayed, "I will sacrifice unto thee with the voice of thanksgiving; I will pay that that I have vowed. Salvation is of the LORD" (Jon. 2:9). And at that, the Lord spoke to the fish and it vomited Jonah unto dry ground.

The book of Jonah in the Bible ends with Jonah angry at God's compassion and refusing to trust the wisdom of the Lord. Jonah was in yet another situation in which he should have entered a time of fasting and prayer. We don't know, however, if he did so.

AN ONGOING DISCIPLINE OF PERIODIC FASTING

The Bible mentions several people who devoted themselves to periodic, perhaps even frequent, times of fasting and prayer. The Gospels say this about John the Baptist: "For John came neither eating nor drinking, and they say, He hath a devil" (Matt. 11:18; Luke 7:33). Some translations specify that the word "eating" in this verse refers to eating bread or grains. The drinking refers to wine. John the Baptist apparently had a pattern in his life of abstaining from grain and wine.

The apostle Paul was also apparently a man who fasted frequently. The Bible says this about him:

- "And he was three days without sight, and neither did eat nor drink" (Acts 9:9). This refers to the days immediately after Paul, called Saul at the time, had an encounter with Jesus while traveling on the road from Jerusalem to Damascus. Paul had seen a vision of intense light and heard the voice of the Lord, and in the aftermath of this, had become blind until the Holy Spirit led a man named Ananias to pray for his sight to be restored three days later. Between the time of Saul's dramatic conversion experience and the prayers of Ananias, Saul did not eat or drink anything.
- "We then, as workers together with him, beseech you also that ye receive not the grace of God in vain. . . . Giving no offence in any thing, that the ministry be not blamed: but in all things approving ourselves as the ministers of God, in much patience, in afflictions, in necessities, in distresses, in stripes, in imprisonments, in tumults, in labours, in watchings, in fastings; by pureness, by knowledge, by longsuffering, by kindness, by the Holy Ghost, by love unfeigned" (2 Cor. 6:1, 3–6). Paul was encouraging the Christians in Corinth to live righteous lives and be worthy witnesses of

the Lord Jesus Christ. He listed some of the ways in which he and his associates had worked as ministers in their midst. He included fasting among the hallmarks of his ministry.

- "In weariness and painfulness, in watchings often, in hunger and thirst, in fastings often, in cold and nakedness" (2 Cor. 11:27). In this passage of Paul's letter to the Corinthians, he was describing his qualifications for ministry to people who had begun to question whether Paul was truly a close follower of Christ Jesus. Paul stated that he fasted often. We don't know how often, or in what ways Paul fasted, but we do know that he fasted and that he was a man of intense and frequent prayer.

In my personal life, I have kept a pattern of fasting through several decades now. As I've mentioned, I fast seven meals a week. This has been an important discipline for me. Fasting has kept me focused on the work of the ministry that the Lord has set before me. It has kept me increasingly reliant upon the Lord to lead and guide my every step. It has given me a much more intense focus on prayer.

I don't know how the Lord will lead you in fasting and praying, but again, the point is not how often or regularly you fast. The key to fasting and praying is to follow the lead of the Holy Spirit in your life. Do what He leads you to do!

7

PRACTICAL TIPS
ABOUT FASTING

God always deals with us where we are to take us where He wants us to be. You need to address a few practical concerns before you begin a fast. God wants you to use wisdom in fasting, and if you are not able physically or mentally to fast at this time, God knows that and He is at work in your life nonetheless.

Recognize that your body is unique and that your approach to fasting must take into consideration your needs and circumstances.

While physicians and other health-care professionals generally agree that fasting can have a beneficial effect on the body, some people should avoid fasting or modify their fasting in some ways. Following is a partial list of those who probably should avoid fasting. If you have any question about whether fasting is appropriate for you, consult your physician before fasting.

THOSE WHO SHOULD AVOID OR MODIFY THEIR FASTING

- Cardiac patients (including those with a weak heart, an irregular heartbeat, artery or valve malfunctions, congestive heart failure, and other conditions).

- Those with a suppressed immune system or who are battling an autoimmune disease.
- Women who are pregnant or nursing (or who think they may be pregnant).
- Those who are preparing for or are recovering from surgery.
- Cancer patients.
- Those who have ulcers.
- Those who suffer from mental illness.
- Diabetics.
- Those who suffer from acute or chronic fatigue.
- Underweight or morbidly obese people.
- Those with low blood pressure.
- Those who are malnourished.
- Those who live or work in extreme cold.

Be aware that some people who are under a great deal of stress may have a suppressed immune system and not know it. If you are suffering from repeated colds or infections, check with your physician about ways to build up your immunity.

Also be aware that overly prolonged fasting can deplete the body of important nutrients, especially vitamins and minerals, and in turn, can cause weakness or malnutrition. (Before commencing a fast, you should assess your health and consider visiting a health professional.)

If you experience a symptom or condition that worsens while you are fasting or that comes on suddenly and severely—such as fainting, bleeding, heart arrhythmias, or other abnormalities—discontinue fasting and consult a physician.

START BEFORE YOU START

Your time of fasting should begin before you ever miss a meal. Take a few days before you fast to eliminate certain foods and habits from your diet. A successful fast generally begins before you ever miss a meal.

Stage 1

Eliminate caffeine, sugar, red meats, dairy products, eggs, and nutritional supplements (when possible) for several days. The same is true for alcohol. Alcoholic beverages are extremely high in sugar and calories, and excessive amounts of alcohol can poison the brain. Do not drink alcohol for at least two weeks before you start a fast, and do not drink it during a fast or in a time of reentry after a fast.

Stage 2

Limit your diet to fruits and vegetables for three to four days to help gradually eliminate harmful substances that promote obesity-related diseases from your body, and easing the body's adjustment during the fasting period. As a part of Stage 2, I recommend this recipe for a "cleansing" soup. You may eat only this soup for three to four days, or eat this soup in addition to vegetables and fruits, especially berries and melons (do not eat bananas). Drink unsweetened herbal tea, cranberry juice, or plain water. This is a wonderful plan for flushing toxins out of your body.

"CLEANSING" SOUP

6 large green onions (scallions—or regular onions)
2 green peppers
1 or 2 large cans of tomatoes
1 bunch of celery
1 large head of cabbage
1 package of Lipton Onion dry soup mix

Season with salt, pepper, curry, parsley, or other spices—or, if desired, use 6 bouillon cubes.

Cut the vegetables in small to medium pieces and cover them with water. Boil fast for ten minutes. Reduce heat to a simmer and continue cooking until vegetables are tender.

You may eat as much as you want of this soup anytime you are hungry—at any time of the day. This soup will not add many calories—in fact, the more you eat of this soup, the more weight you are likely to lose because the ingredients in this soup take more calories to digest than are present in the ingredients.

You may fill a Thermos with this soup and take it with you during the day. The soup at home can be kept hot in a Crock-Pot or slow cooker.

DON'T BE SURPRISED IF . . .

For many people, fasting has some fairly common physical symptoms that may be unusual compared to a person's norm. These physical symptoms may include headache; a coated tongue; bad breath; fatigue; irritability; dizziness; light-headedness; changes in digestion, urine, or stools; skin eruptions; heightened emotions; or even a detectable body odor. In most cases, these effects diminish after the first few days of a fast as the body is cleansed from the inside out.

As uncomfortable—or unpleasant—symptoms recede, you may notice an increased energy level, improved mental clarity and alertness, and an uplifted attitude and renewed motivation. You may even develop a healthier approach to eating. Many people have a longing for simply prepared and whole foods—such as whole pieces of fruit and raw vegetables. These foods often seem to be more satisfying after a fast. Some people have reported a heightened sense of taste after a fast—they truly are able to enjoy foods in their natural, uncombined, unprocessed, unrefined state.

FOUR PRACTICALITIES

Here are four very practical suggestions as you fast:

1. Drink Lots of Water

Strictly speaking, fasting means abstaining from everything except water. Even though other beverages may be calorie-free, you are better off avoiding them. Some no-calorie beverages actually contain chemicals that have been proven harmful to the body and brain over time. Coffee and tea stimulate the central nervous system at a time when you are trying to give your body a rest. Drinks that are artificially colored and flavored often bring up a memory of food and arouse hunger more than they quench hunger. Stick to water!

You may, of course, drink mineral water. In fact, I recommend it. Distilled water is pure, but it has zero mineral content. Ordinary tap water often contains chlorine and may contain fluorides—at the very least—and the taste of these chemical additives can be offensive.

Water helps flush toxins and waste material from the body. As a person fasts, the body begins to use stored fuel fat cells for energy. Waste by-products are produced in this process and must be cleansed from the body. Water is the best cleansing agent. Water also helps to calm any hunger pangs that occur at the beginning of a fast.

Water (fortified with electrolytes) also helps greatly with any muscle cramping that a person might experience during a fast. When the body begins to draw fat that has been stored in muscle cells, muscles can cramp a little. If you begin to feel any cramping, perhaps in your legs at night, drink water or another beverage that is fortified with electrolytes. In most cases, that will ease the cramps within a few minutes.

I recommend that you drink at least two quarts of water (fortified with electrolytes) every day of a fast, but there really is no limit to the amount of water you may drink. Some in the medical world recommend that even a nonfasting person drink two or more quarts of water a day, depending on the person's weight.

Avoid drinking water that is too cold. Warm or room-temperature water is best.

2. Exercise Moderately

Contrary to what many people believe, exercise does not stimulate appetite. Rather, researchers have found that an hour of exercise a day actually reduces appetite. The body burns up calories faster when we exercise, and it continues to burn calories at an accelerated pace for as long as twenty-four hours after an exercise hour.

As you fast you may not feel like doing strenuous exercises, and you probably should not exercise vigorously. Avoid jogging or distance running. You may not want to participate in strenuous sports activities, such as playing soccer. Taking a long walk, doing stretches for flexibility, swimming laps, riding a bicycle, and doing lightweight training are all good forms of exercise during a fast. There certainly is no reason why you can't play golf or go bowling or participate in other sports that are a little less strenuous.

I usually recommend to people who are fasting that they walk up to an hour a day if at all possible. This is a wonderful time to pray! (Before commencing a fast, you should assess your health and consider visiting a health professional.)

3. Eliminate as Many Food Cues as Possible

It seems that once a person starts fasting, he sees every billboard, every restaurant sign, and every television commercial with new eyes. Every radio commercial seems to be about food. The whole world suddenly seems based on food, with the intent of enticing a person to eat more and drink more!

As much as possible, remove these cues from your life. Refuse to look at billboards and fast food restaurant signs. Turn off the television set and radio. In some cases, you may want to get away for a while to a place where you can rest— perhaps getting out of a city and into a small town in the mountains.

Stay away from areas where you know the aroma of food will trigger hunger. One man told me that he took a new route to work when he started fasting and praying because his old route took him by a bakery that produced yeast-bread products. The area was filled with the aroma of rising and baking bread, and he knew that this aroma would trigger feelings of hunger in him.

If you are in a retreat center or at a resort or spa during your time of fasting and prayer, stay away from the dining rooms and buffet tables.

Don't tempt yourself by keeping candy, bowls of nuts, or other foods around your house or within easy reach.

Most people pray during the time they would normally eat a meal or snack. I believe it is also important to have activities to do during the times in which you would normally shop for food or spend time preparing food. Prayer may be one of those activities, but other appropriate activities are reading your Bible, writing in a journal, or writing a letter of encouragement to a friend in need. Keeping your mind busy during a time of fasting—off food and on to other things—is very helpful.

4. Take Your Prescription Medications

You should continue to take prescribed medications as you fast—as well as before a fast and as you reenter eating after a fast. (People with diabetes or other chronic illnesses should ask their doctors how to modify their medications during a fast, and how frequently to monitor their blood sugar.)

ENDING YOUR FAST WISELY

Ending a fast is a little like landing a jet airplane. How you "come down" is critical to a safe arrival! Your body needs a gentle transition to normal eating. The longer the fast, the longer the reentry period should be. Usually, a transition time of about half the length of the fast will enable the body to safely gear up to handle a full complement of food groups.

Reentry Stage 1

Gradually introduce unsweetened and highly diluted fruit juices to your body. Gradually increase a stronger concentration over several days.

Reentry Stage 2

Watery vegetables that are easy to digest—vegetables very low in starch—can be added to fruit juices. Spinach, zucchini squash, and other greens are good choices.

Reentry Stage 3

Add well-cooked brown rice or millet in small quantities.

Reentry Stage 4

Nuts, seeds, or beans can be added.

Reentry Stage 5

Richer protein foods—meat, fish, poultry, and dairy products—should be the final additions during your transition. This is also true for whole-grain breads and pasta, potatoes, and all starches other than the rice and millet in Stage 3.

As you end a time of fasting, be sure to chew solid foods thoroughly. Saliva contains enzymes that begin the digestive process before food reaches the stomach. This gives your stomach a chance to get back to speed. It reduces the potential for trauma to the digestive system and keeps you from having blockages.

If you return to normal eating too quickly, you can cause short-term symptoms such as nausea and vomiting. In extreme cases, people have injured their internal organs, and in rare cases, death has resulted.

Before commencing a fast, you should assess your health and consider visiting a health professional.

Marilyn Hickey Ministries acknowledges and embraces the numerous references found in the Old and New Testament to the practice of fasting. We believe that Christ encouraged fasting for His disciples, and for us, through His example. We believe that the purpose of periodic fasting is to accompany prayer, but we do not believe that there is a biblical *requirement* or instruction for everyone to participate in fasting. Christ, in Scripture, distinguished between appropriate and inappropriate times for fasting.

As in all other aspects of your relationship with God, you should make a decision to participate in fasting only after taking into consideration whether fasting is appropriate for you as an individual—apart from and without any involvement in a group that may be fasting. We encourage you to thoroughly confirm your spiritual and physical suitability before fasting for any period of time. Carefully consider your personal health condition, contraindications of any medicines you may be taking, as well as the appropriate fasting procedures and measures to conclude a fast. These factors are the responsibility of the individual. We always recommend that a person consult his or her physician before a strict or prolonged fast.

PART II

GOD'S PURPOSES FOR OUR FASTING AND PRAYING

THE FASTS GOD HONORS

One of the most important passages in the Bible about fasting is found in Isaiah 58. God gave His people a message about how and why not to fast, and about why to fast. The Lord began by pointing out the wrong motivations for fasting. In speaking about the priests in the temple, the Lord said through the prophet Isaiah:

> They seek me daily, and delight to know my ways, as a nation that did righteousness, and forsook not the ordinance of their God: they ask of me the ordinances of justice; they take delight in approaching to God.
>
> Where have we fasted, say they, and thou seest not? Wherefore have we afflicted our soul, and thou takest no knowledge? Behold, in the day of your fast ye find pleasure, and exact all your labours.
>
> Behold, ye fast for strife and debate, and to smite with the fist of wickedness: ye shall not fast as ye do this day, to make your voice to be heard on high.
>
> Is it such a fast that I have chosen? A day for a man to afflict his soul? Is it to bow down his head as a bulrush, and to spread sackcloth and ashes under him? Wilt thou call this a fast, and an acceptable day to the LORD? (Isaiah 58: 2–5)

What was the Lord saying to His people? First, He was chiding His people for coming before Him as if everything was all right in their lives. The priests were seeking His will and asking for His justice—with an assumption that they were doing what was required of them. They were coming with a presumption that God owed them not only answers, but blessings. They had a false understanding of their own goodness.

Second, the Lord was calling His people to recognize that their motives for fasting had been all wrong. They were "finding pleasure" in fasting. In other words, they were fasting so they could tell others they had fasted. They were also fasting so they could feel justified in having others do their work—in some cases, "exacting labour" on their behalf, requiring that others work so they could devote themselves to doing something religious, and therefore, of greater value.

Third, the Lord was calling His people to recognize that their behavior while they were fasting is wrong. They were quarreling and debating with one another, rather than seeking ways in which they might come together before the Lord.

Fourth and finally, the Lord was calling His people to understand that the outward signs and behaviors associated with fasting—a bowed head and the wearing of sackcloth and ashes—were not what fasting is all about. Fasting is a matter of the heart, not a matter of outward appearances.

In all these ways, the people were attempting to do something religious in order to manipulate God into hearing and answering their selfish petitions. The Lord made it very clear that this was unacceptable in His eyes.

We need to be careful that we don't fall into the same traps.

WHAT GOD DOES NOT WANT

Fasting does not put us into right relationship with God. It doesn't save us or empower us in and of itself. Jesus Christ saves us. The Holy Spirit empowers us. Fasting puts us into a position to recognize our own need of a Savior and for more of the Holy Spirit's work in our lives. Fasting is a humbling experience, not an exalting experience. God never desires that a person fast in order to be saved or as an alternative approach to receiving Jesus Christ as Savior.

God doesn't give religious gold stars to the person who fasts. We must never make a point of prideful boasting that we went on a fast with our church or Bible study. We must never think that our fasting brought about a miracle. God is the worker of miracles. Fasting is a means of putting us into a position to trust God more and to rely upon God to do His work in us, through us, and all around us. There's no magic in fasting and we must never think that fasting makes us better than other Christians who don't fast.

Fasting calls a person to a humbling of the spirit, not just a humbling of the body. Fasting is always aimed at deepening a person's relationship with God. It is not a trapping of religion, but rather, a means of bringing about greater trust in the Lord.

So what is God's purpose in calling us to fast?

GOD'S TWELVEFOLD PURPOSE FOR FASTING

In speaking to His people through the prophet Isaiah, the Lord then turned toward the purpose of fasting. He described the fast that He had chosen for His people. I encourage you to read this passage slowly and carefully:

Is not this the fast that I have chosen? To loose the bands of wickedness, to undo the heavy burdens, and to let the oppressed go free, and that ye break every yoke?

Is it not to deal thy bread to the hungry, and that thou bring the poor that are cast out to thy house? When thou seest the naked, that thou cover him; and that thou hide not thyself from thine own flesh?

Then shall thy light break forth as the morning, and thine health shall spring forth speedily; and thy righteousness shall go before thee; the glory of the LORD shall be thy rearward.

Then shalt thou call, and the LORD shall answer; thou shalt cry, and he shall say, Here I am. If thou take away from the midst of thee the yoke, the putting forth of the finger, and speaking vanity; and if thou draw out thy soul to the hungry, and satisfy the afflicted soul; then shall thy light rise in obscurity, and thy darkness be as the noon day: and the LORD shall guide thee continually, and satisfy thy soul in drought, and make fat thy bones: and thou shalt be like a watered garden, and like a spring of water, whose waters fail not.

And they that shall be of thee shall build the old waste places: thou shalt raise up the foundations of many generations; and thou shalt be called, The repairer of the breach, The restorer of paths to dwell in. (Isaiah 58:6–12)

This passage identifies twelve specific purposes for fasting. Let me list and explain each of them to you, knowing that whatever the Scriptures identify in lists like these has both natural and spiritual dimensions. The Lord was calling His people to take beneficial and specific actions that were outward, visible, and measurable. At the same time, the Lord was calling His people to experience emotional and spiritual benefits that were internal and eternal.

1. Loose the Bands of Wickedness

Evil puts its victims in a vise. We sometimes say that a person is "in the grip of evil." To loose the bands of wickedness means to confront evil and to be set free from any hold the devil might have on your life. The "bands of wickedness" refers very specifically to such things as addictions, entrenched sinful habits, and spiritual strongholds. The Lord desires that we be set free—that these bands be taken from our lives so we can experience life freely and in its fullness.

In the time of the Israelites, wickedness was most commonly associated with the worship of false idols. To be wicked was to fail to worship Jehovah as the one true and living God Almighty. Wickedness in our lives also involves trusting in something other than God. The person who is bound up by wickedness is a person whose first thought every morning is how he can feed an addiction, practice a sinful habit, or exact revenge. The wicked person is bound up in a false perception of reality—he has bought into a lie about who God is, and that lie keeps him from responding to God's love, forgiveness, and mercy.

A person who has been bound up by wickedness needs to be delivered.

2. Undo the Heavy Burdens

Many people walk today under heavy burdens. A person who is burdened feels weighed down by something, slowed, incapable of moving freely. Some burdens are self-imposed. Some people or circumstances beyond our control place burdens upon us. Some burdens exist in the natural—such as the burden of debt. Some burdens are spiritual—such as concern for an unsaved child or a seriously ill loved one. The Lord desires that the heavy burdens be lifted from us, and He makes that possible.

The person with a heavy burden needs to have a way out from under the burden, and that way out is usually going to involve sharing of the load with other people or lightening the load by giving up something.

3. Let the Oppressed Go Free

There are many forms of oppression today. Oppressed people are trapped in situations from which they see no out. Oppression is a spiritual condition—it is rooted in pressing doubts and in feelings of depression and despair. Oppressed people have no hope, they have very little joy, and they nearly always are low in faith.

The oppressed person needs to lift up his eyes to the Lord and see that the Lord has made a way where there seemed to be no way.

4. Break Every Yoke

A yoke is a device that constrains a person to work in a highly prescribed manner by someone in higher authority. A farmer yoked an ox in Bible times so he could compel that ox to move forward and pull a plow. Yokes also linked animals together— for example, two oxen in a yoke with one set of reins.

What constitutes a yoke for a person today? It's generally being in an association, affiliation, or relationship that doesn't fit the Christian. It may mean working in an ungodly environment, having an ungodly business partner, or dating an ungodly person. It can mean being part of a group that constrains you to do something that is outside the talents God has given you and is outside the purposes God has for your life. It can mean being in a situation in which you feel that you must do or undo certain things that you know are wrong in order to stay in a relationship. Those who are in a relationship with abusers are under a heavy yoke.

The person who is yoked to unrighteousness needs to be loosed and set free.

5. Feed the Hungry

What is it that truly satisfies the hungry soul? The nourishment of God's Word. The person who is hungry for truth is a person God delights in feeding. God calls us not only to dig deeper and deeper into His Word, but He also calls us to feed other people the truth. When we take in and then give out God's Word, there's a twofold benefit: Others receive a great blessing in hearing the gospel. We receive a blessing in sharing the gospel.

Feeding the hungry requires learning and teaching. It requires becoming bold in declaring the truth in every situation in which a lie currently prevails.

6. Provide for the Poor

What is it that makes a person poor? Sometimes we experience a lack in our lives because of circumstances beyond our control—for example, an employer may go through bankruptcy, a spouse may die, all available resources might be directed toward helping a sick loved one, or a person might be in the path of a devastating storm or experience a tragic accident. Very often, however, we experience a lack because we have not learned how to receive what God desires us to have. We have a lack of faith . . . a lack of knowledge . . . a lack of understanding . . . a lack of wisdom . . . a lack of compassion.

Providing for the poor requires taking action with our faith and moving into areas of need with God's love.

7. Clothe the Naked

Those who love the Lord Jesus Christ are to be clothed with righteousness. At the heart of this word *righteousness* is the word *right.* To be right means that we are lined up or in alignment in the right ways. As Christians we are to walk out our lives with confidence that we are in right relationship with God, doing the right things in the right timing for the right results.

Clothing the naked requires a checkup of our righteousness.

8. Restore Family Relationships

The Lord said that we were not to "hide [ourselves]" from "our own flesh."

This means that as we seek to feed the hungry, provide for the poor, and clothe the naked, we do that first and foremost in our own families. We come into harmony with other family members through establishing the truth in our relationships, grounding our lives on the Word of God, learning how God desires us to live and then living in that way, and by seeking to do all things in a way that brings God's blessing.

Restoring family relationships requires a willingness to let go of old hurts and patterns and seeking to live in God's love and God's commandments related to the family.

9. Cause Light to Break Forth

God desires for you to be a witness to this world. Jesus said to His followers,

> Ye are the light of the world. A city that is set on an hill cannot be hid. Neither do men light a candle, and put it under a bushel, but on a candlestick; and it giveth light unto all that are in the house. Let your light so shine before men, that they may see your good works, and glorify your Father which is in heaven. (Matthew 5:14–16)

God desires us to so live our lives that people will be drawn to us—they will want to come out of darkness and live in the light of God's love and forgiveness.

To have our "light break forth as the morning," the Lord said through Isaiah, we must be willing to repent of any sin that is acting as a shield or filter to our witness. We must ask the Lord to cleanse us of all sin and negative habits.

10. Bring Healing Speedily

God does not desire for His people to be sick. He said to the Is-raelites, "If thou wilt diligently hearken to the voice of the LORD thy God, and wilt do that which is right in his sight, and wilt give ear to his commandments, and keep all his statutes, I will put none of these diseases upon thee, which I have brought upon the Egyptians: for I am the LORD that healeth thee" (Exod. 15:26). The Egyptians had rebelled against God's Word and had hardened their hearts against God. As a result, they ex-perienced tremendous plagues, most of which were associated with horrible diseases, and finally death.

God's desire for you is health. He desires for you to be strong in your body, soul, and spirit. He desires for you to have all of the energy and strength you need to complete the tasks that He has set before you. He desires for you to live a high-quality life so you might be the best possible witness you can be for Him as long as possible!

To experience God's healing and wholeness speedily means that we turn away from any form of rebellion against God's commandments and that we seek to establish habits in our lives that lead to health, wholeness, and a vibrancy of life.

11. Establish a Path of Righteousness

The Lord has a plan and a purpose for every person's life. There is a path that God intended for you to walk. He gave you specific gifts and talents so that you might walk that particular path with great success in His eyes. God also left it up to you to decide whether you will walk that path. To establish a path that is right before the Lord is to do three things: to determine what God has gifted you to do, to determine when and how you should de-velop those gifts, and to determine where and in what ways God desires for you to use those gifts in service to other people.

To establish a path of righteousness, you need to understand why God has put you on this earth and to embrace God's plan and purpose.

12. See the Glory of the Lord in Results

The Lord does not set up His people for failure. No! God wants you to succeed. He desires that everything you put your hand to prospers. He wants you to reap a thirtyfold, sixtyfold, hundred-fold return on every seed you plant! To have the glory of the Lord as our "rearward"—in the King James language of Isaiah 58:8—means that when we look behind us at what God has done in us and through us, we see great cause to give praise and thanksgiving. We have a new understanding that God is in control of all things, and that God honors His Word and is faithful all the time.

GREAT REWARDS FOR FASTING AS THE LORD DESIRES

The Lord continued in His prophecy through Isaiah that God would give great rewards to those who fulfilled the fasts to which God had called His people:

- When they called upon Him, the Lord would answer.
- The Lord would take away from them all bondage, all accusations, and all pride.
- The Lord would increase their reputation and visibility.
- The Lord would guide them continually.
- The Lord would satisfy their souls—He would meet all of their emotional needs for love, value, and purpose.
- The Lord would give them renewed health and vitality.
- The Lord would restore what had been destroyed or obliterated in their lives.
- The Lord would raise up new generations who would look back on them and bless the heritage they had established.

- They would know the delight of the Lord's presence.
- They would be lifted into positions of leadership.

What an incredible, awesome, mighty blessing for God's people who completed the fast of the Lord!

In the remaining chapters of this book we are going to take a deeper look at each of the twelve purposes in fasting. For each purpose in fasting, God has provided one or more examples in His Word. We'll also take a look at the role of prayer in each of these fasts.

EXAMINE YOUR OWN HEART

At the close of this chapter, I encourage you to go back and read Isaiah 58:1–4. Ask yourself these questions:

- *Do I feel any real need to fast, or do I think that everything is all right in my life? Am I willing to admit there's an area in which I need a breakthrough? Is there a sorrow in my life that God wants me to address in a time of prayer and fasting?*
- *What is my real motive for fasting? Is it to draw closer to God or to draw attention to myself for being a person who deprives himself, does the religiously difficult thing, or puts on an outward show of piety?*
- *What is it I desire most from God? What is keeping me from receiving what I desire?*

PRAYING AND FASTING TO OVERCOME EVIL

Four of the main purposes to fast in Isaiah 58 are these:

1. Loosing the bands of wickedness.
2. Undoing the heavy burdens.
3. Letting the oppressed go free.
4. Breaking every yoke.

Each of these reasons to fast and pray is aimed at breaking the bonds of evil on a person's life, a loved one's life, or on a body of believers, including a family, church, or ministry. In each case, the time spent in fasting and praying is a time devoted to seeking God's power to bring deliverance.

In this section, we'll deal with each of these purposes for fasting, with an emphasis placed on your prayers as you pursue God's plan for overcoming evil.

8

LOOSING THE BANDS OF WICKEDNESS

Wickedness is not a word that we hear used a great deal in our world today, yet virtually everybody seems to know what it means. Something that is wicked is very bad, and it causes or has the potential to cause something that is very harmful or distressing.

When we fast and pray to loose the bands of wickedness, we need to address those things that are very wrong in our lives. We are addressing what causes us the most harm. And what is it that is the most deadly to us, not just physically but spiritually? It is sin. The apostle Paul wrote to the Romans: "For the wages of sin is death; but the gift of God is eternal life through Jesus Christ our Lord" (Rom. 6:23).

The Bible mentions sin countless times, especially if you count all of the references to ungodly behavior, evil, trespasses, and specific behaviors that everybody agrees are sinful. The Bible has a number of lists of sins, which identify everything from murder to gossip, adultery to lying, stealing to anger (see Gal. 5:19–21 for one such list). We might consider the Ten Commandments a list of what God regards as the top ten sins to avoid (see Exod. 20:1–17). Perhaps the greatest of the sins is related to the first commandment: "I am the LORD thy God, which have brought thee out of the land of Egypt, out of the house of bondage. Thou shalt have no other gods before me" (Exod. 20:2–3).

All sin, however, is part of the first and foremost sin: unbelief. If a person refuses to believe in God . . . refuses to believe that he must keep God's commandments . . . refuses to believe that all sin is punishable, even to the point of death . . . refuses to believe that God can redeem and cleanse him from sin . . . that person cannot be saved. Unbelief is at the root of all sin.

Jesus recognized this in one particular experience. Jesus had gone into the mountains with three of His disciples for a time of fasting and prayer. There, He was transfigured in their presence. It was a spiritually high moment for Peter, James, and John. When Jesus and these three disciples descended the mountain, they found the other disciples of Jesus dealing with a man whose son was demon-possessed. The story is found in the Gospel of Matthew:

> And when they were come to the multitude, there came to him a certain man, kneeling down to him, and saying, Lord, have mercy on my son: for he is lunatick, and sore vexed: for ofttimes he falleth into the fire, and oft into the water. And I brought him to thy disciples, and they could not cure him.
>
> Then Jesus answered and said, O faithless and perverse generation, how long shall I be with you? How long shall I suffer you? Bring him hither to me.
>
> And Jesus rebuked the devil; and he was departed out of him: and the child was cured from that very hour.
>
> Then came the disciples to Jesus apart, and said, Why could not we cast him out?
>
> And Jesus said unto them, Because of your unbelief: for verily I say unto you, If ye have faith as a grain of mustard seed, ye shall say unto this mountain, Remove

hence to yonder place; and it shall remove; and nothing
shall be impossible unto you. Howbeit this kind goeth
not out but by prayer and fasting. (Matthew 17:14–21)

THE DISCIPLES' FAST

The prayer and fasting time to which Jesus called His disciples
in this passage has often been called the "disciples' fast." There is
no time frame associated with it. This is a time of praying and
fasting that amounts to "as long as it takes."

Most people want deliverance quickly. They want to be able
to fast for one meal and pray for five minutes, then have the
Lord strip away addictions or sinful habits from their lives immediately, even though those addictions or habits may have
been engrained in their lives for decades. Certainly the Lord can
and does deliver people instantly. At other times the Lord delivers a person over a period of time.

Do not be discouraged if your deliverance doesn't come
quickly. Press on! Continue to fast and pray as the Lord leads
you. At the same time, be open at every hour of your fasting for
the Lord to set you free. God is not bound by time as we often
are bound in our own thinking. God is concerned with results
that are for your eternal benefit, not only your health and
wholeness on this earth. He is committed to loosing you from a
band of wickedness in such a way that the band never returns
again to your life.

Rather, you are set free, renewed, and strengthened to walk
forward in life, trusting the Holy Spirit to empower you every
day to say no to your past behavior and thought life.

Confronting the Core Issue of Unbelief

Jesus indicated clearly that the bands of wickedness that held
this young man in their grip were bands that could not be

loosed until he addressed the issue of unbelief. He plainly told His disciples that they had been unable to cast out the evil spirits from this boy because of their unbelief. He pointed directly to prayer and fasting as a means of developing and activating their faith.

Many people today are bound by bands of wickedness. Most know that they are bound, some don't. Those who are addicted are bound. Those who are entrenched in repeated sinful habits are bound. Those who are filled with obsessive thoughts and compulsive behaviors are bound. And at the core of each of these very prevalent conditions is a kernel of unbelief.

Generally speaking, people who are in denial about an addiction, sinful habit, obsession, or compulsive behavior are doubly bound because they refuse to believe they have a problem! Not only do they have unbelief about the cause, nature, and solution for their problem, they have unbelief about the very existence of the problem.

At the core of unbelief are these assumptions:

- God has nothing to do with my problem—either He isn't interested in me or my problems, or He is incapable of helping me with my problem.
- I don't need any help. I can handle my problem by myself.

Because of these assumptions, the person who is bound by wickedness finds him- or herself trusting someone or something instead of God when it comes to dealing with a situation that can cause real damage, even death.

A pastor once told me how God had called him to Louisville a number of years ago. He contacted one of the most spiritually gifted men in our nation at that time, William Branham. He asked Branham, "Should I go to Louisville? I feel like the Lord is calling me there."

Branham answered, "Don't go there. That place is simply

overpowered with darkness—the worst place in the United States to go. It is a graveyard for preachers."

The man returned to the Lord and prayed, "Lord, here is a man of God saying not to go."

The Lord said, "But I'm telling you to go."

He went, and Branham later called him and said, "I told you my opinion, but after praying for you, God told me He had sent you there." The man was a pastor in that city for about ten years, and he didn't seem to accomplish anything. Things looked really bad; the church was not doing well.

This pastor went to Chicago to apply for another church without telling his people about it. While he was in Chicago, the Lord spoke to him and said, "What are you doing here? I called you to Louisville."

The pastor answered, "God, I'm failing in Louisville! I'm tired of Louisville. I've tried everything for ten years and nothing works, so I'm going to change."

God said, "You'll be out of My will."

He said, "I must not be in Your will there!"

Then God said, "You're in My will, but you need to go back and call your church to fasting and prayer." So this man began a tremendous prayer program, and within two years his church grew from two hundred people to two thousand people.

What made the difference? Obedience to God in prayer and fasting had broken the powers of darkness over that city. The powers of darkness were there from the beginning, but the pastor had done nothing necessary to break the force of those powers for ten years. Sometimes we must fast and pray to break the powers of darkness and see unbelief turned into the revival power of belief.

The truth of God's Word is that God cares about every problem we have. God desires to deliver us from all forms of evil, including self-inflicted bad habits. God is capable of delivering us, and we need His delivering power.

PREPARING FOR THIS FAST

The way we come to a time of praying and fasting for release from the bands of wickedness is this:

First, we acknowledge that something is very wrong. We must deal with it before we experience even worse consequences than the ones we may already be experiencing.

Second, we ask God to show us the root of our problem. On the surface, the problem may appear to be one thing—but if we dig deeper, the problem may actually be something quite different. For example, a number of people who are addicted to various substances—from alcohol to sugar, from fats to prescription medications—find in a time of praying and fasting that the real issue in their lives is whether God loves and values them. When people don't acknowledge the love of God toward them—which gives their lives tremendous meaning, purpose, and value—they look to other things or people for comfort and love. They begin to rely on themselves for self-value and self-love, or they turn to someone or some substance they believe will bolster their worth and give them greater feelings of acceptance.

Third, we must ask God to help us reject and replace the lie that is at the core of the wickedness we are experiencing with His truth. We must be quick to say to the Lord:

- "I accept Your love."
- "I accept Your forgiveness."
- "I accept Your mercy."
- "I acknowledge my need of Your help."
- "I choose to believe that You will deliver me from this bondage, and that You are delivering me."

Confronting a Besetting Sin

The Bible refers to the "sin which so easily doth beset us," or *besetting sins* (Heb. 12:1). These are not sins of neglect or momentary lapses in good behavior. These are sins that have an element of rebellion to them. The person who has given in to a besetting sin is a person who says, "I shall" even though he knows God has said, "Thou shalt not." The rebellious person begins to sin with a feeling that he can handle the sin, and if there should be any negative consequences, he can handle them. The truth is, nobody can handle the consequences of sin.

As you begin to fast and pray for the bands of wickedness to be loosed, you must acknowledge your inability to deliver yourself. You must own up to the rebellion that led initially into the behavior that resulted in an addiction, sinful habit, obsession, or compulsion.

Ask the Lord to forgive you for thinking that you could control your own life. Ask Him to forgive you for relying on your own strength.

Believing for God's Best

As you pray and fast, make a conscious decision that you are going to believe God will act in your life or the life of your loved one. You may want to write down your expectation with a simple sentence: "I believe God will. . . ."

As you write out what you are trusting God to do in your life, acknowledge before the Lord that He also desires the very best in your life and that He has made a way for you to be delivered. The Bible tells us, "There hath no temptation taken you but such as is common to man: but God is faithful, who will not suffer you to be tempted above that ye are able; but will with the temptation also make a way to escape, that ye may be able to bear it" (1 Cor. 10:13).

You may be able to put your expectation into one sentence, or you may have several sentences that state what you desire God to do. Keep this statement in your Bible and refer to it often during your time of prayer and fasting.

Anticipating the Devil's Lies

Usually you can count on the devil to come back around to whisper to you the lies that trapped you in wickedness in the first place. He is likely to say:

- "This isn't going to work."
- "Nothing is going to change."
- "There's nothing that you or anybody, including God, can do about this."
- "God doesn't really care what you eat [or smoke, drink, or take]."
- "If you don't continue in this behavior [addiction, habit, obsession, compulsive behavior], you will be worse off than you are right now."
- "Your behavior [addiction, habit, obsession, compulsive behavior] is so deep in your life that God cannot forgive you and will not help you. You have worn out God's patience and gone beyond the extent of His mercy."

Lies, lies, and more lies! Reject these thoughts as they come to your mind, which they may do especially as you begin a fast and are in a weakened physical state. Fight off these lies with prayers that are rooted in what you believe and what you are expecting from God. Remind the devil that he is a liar and the father of all lies, and that you are praying and fasting because you are believing for the truth of God to be established in your life.

PRAYING TO RELEASE THE ENEMY'S HOLD

In going to the Bible and praying what the Bible says, you are speaking the truth of God into your situation and into your own heart and mind. Let me encourage you to pray into your life these Bible verses. Note that in some cases, the verses refer to enemies. Let me assure you: your addiction, entrapping habit, obsession, or compulsion is an enemy to you. You must speak the truth of God to your own heart!

- The LORD is my rock, and my fortress, and my deliverer; the God of my rock; in him will I trust: he is my shield, and the horn of my salvation, my high tower, and my refuge, my saviour; thou savest me from violence. I will call on the LORD, who is worthy to be praised: so shall I be saved from mine enemies. (2 Samuel 22:2–4)
- The LORD is my rock, and my fortress, and my deliverer; my God, my strength, in whom I will trust; my buckler, and the horn of my salvation, and my high tower. (Psalm 18:2)
- I am poor and needy; yet the Lord thinketh upon me: thou art my help and my deliverer; make no tarrying, O my God. (Psalm 40:17)
- I am poor and needy: make haste unto me, O God: thou art my help and my deliverer; O LORD, make no tarrying. (Psalm 70:5)
- Quicken me, O LORD, for thy name's sake: for thy righteousness' sake bring my soul out of trouble. (Psalm 143:11)

Praise and Thanksgiving for Your Deliverance

Accompany your times of prayer with heavy doses of praise and thanksgiving for who God is and what God has done and promised to do for you. Let me give you some examples of praise and thanksgiving statements.

- "Heavenly Father, thank You for keeping me alive to this day. Thank You that I haven't died in my addiction [my bad habit, my obsession or compulsion]. Thank You that You still have a purpose for my being on this earth."

- "Heavenly Father, thank You that You have led me to this time of fasting and praying so that I might experience Your healing and delivering power in a new way."
- "Heavenly Father, thank You for providing for me all that I need. Thank You for loving me, forgiving me, and healing me."
- "I praise You, Lord, that You are my Savior and my Deliverer."
- "I praise You, Lord, that You are my Healer."
- "I praise You, Lord, that Your very nature is love and that You love me with an everlasting love."
- "I praise You, Lord, that You have made a way for me to live and that You are the one who created me for health and wholeness, not an addiction [a habit that you can't change, compulsive behaviors, or obsessive ideas]."

Pray Specifically for Deliverance

Pray for your own deliverance, asking the Lord, "Heavenly Father, please deliver me from evil. Deliver me from these cravings and recurring ideas that I can't seem to overcome or control. Give me Your strength and Your power to withstand the temptations that come to me. Deliver me!" Name your problem to the Lord and voice your belief that God desires to deliver you, God is in the process of delivering you, and that the mighty and incomparable Almighty God will deliver you.

9

UNDOING HEAVY BURDENS

Every person has difficult times in life. There's no way of avoiding all problems, and this is true for Christians as well as non-Christians. Job, probably the oldest book in the Bible, says, "Man that is born of a woman is of few days, and full of trouble" (14:1). People age. Storms come. Financial markets rise and fall. Houses need to be refurbished over time and cars need to be fixed up or replaced. At times, the problems become extreme.

The person who has a heavy burden feels weighed down by life's problems. He is often discouraged to the point of feeling depressed. Rather than feeling on top of things, he feels under the gun, down in the depths, under stress.

Some of the foremost burdens in the natural realm of our lives are related to financial debt. Others are related to taking on too many obligations to produce a quality result in too little time . . . or taking on too many responsibilities for the care of others. Still other burdens are related to poor health, perhaps a major disease in a person's own body or in the body of a loved one.

In the spirit realm, people often feel burdened out of concern for loved ones who have not yet accepted Jesus Christ as their Savior.

Not every burden we experience is of our own doing. Sometimes people or circumstances place burdens upon us.

The Bible gives us an example of people who fasted when they were under a heavy burden. The story is found in Ezra 8.

THE FAST CALLED BY EZRA

The book of Ezra tells the story of Jews who were traveling after years of captivity in Persia. King Cyrus of Persia had given them permission to rebuild the temple. The first wave of people returned to Jerusalem under the leadership of a man named Zerubbabel. The work was slow going but after twenty-three years, the people had rebuilt the temple.

Ezra, a priest, led a second band of people to Jerusalem, including a large contingent of priests, to resume the various rituals and sacrifices of the temple. The king gave Ezra and his group a large sum of money to beautify and outfit the temple. As the people arrived at the Ahava River, Ezra realized he had a major problem. His group was about to cross an area where bands of nomads routinely robbed travelers and took them into slavery. Ezra and his group were very vulnerable to attack—they were unskilled and unarmed. We read in Ezra 8:21–22:

> Then I proclaimed a fast there, at the river of Ahava, that we might afflict ourselves before our God, to seek of him a right way for us, and for our little ones, and for all our substance. For I was ashamed to require of the king a band of soldiers and horsemen to help us against the enemy in the way: because we had spoken unto the king, saying, The hand of our God is upon all them for good that seek him; but his power and his wrath is against all them that forsake him.

Ezra was burdened. He had told the king that God took care of those who truly worshiped Him, but suddenly he found himself needing very practical assistance and no armed soldiers were present to escort his defenseless people to Jerusalem.

The people fasted and sought God in prayer . . . and God gave Ezra a plan for how to complete the journey.

Those who are burdened need a plan from God. In Ezra's case, the plan was for Ezra to separate out twelve of the priests and to disperse among them the silver, gold, and vessels for the temple. The people sought God in prayer for their protection, and the Bible tells us, "The hand of our God was upon us, and he delivered us from the hand of the enemy, and of such as lay in wait by the way. And we came to Jerusalem" (Ezra 8:31–32).

I stated in an earlier chapter that one of the ways in which to lighten a burden is to share it with other people. The Bible tells us, "Bear ye one another's burdens, and so fulfil the law of Christ" (Gal. 6:2). The person under a heavy burden enjoys great comfort when he calls other people alongside to help carry the load—either in a practical way or in prayer.

At times, however, we need a plan from God for requiring others around us to take on part of the load. In distributing the money and precious vessels to twelve priests, Ezra was not only distributing the physical weight of those metal objects, he was also distributing the responsibility for the safekeeping and care of those items. He was distributing the leadership role. Sometimes we, too, need to divide up a burdensome job or leadership responsibility among others so that not only are the physical chores divided, but also the authority and accountability for getting a job done.

A Burden or a Challenge?

God does not place heavy burdens on us. There are times, however, when God does call us to pursue a particular opportunity, and we may feel that the challenge is beyond our ability. In most cases, this is true! God often calls His people to undertake tasks—especially tasks that win souls and take God's preaching, teaching, and healing ministry to the lost—that are beyond our ability and capacity. That's where faith comes in! God seems to say to us, "I want you to do this. I know the task is bigger than what you can do. I want you to put your total trust in Me to help you."

God desires for us to accomplish great things for His kingdom and in His name, but God does not share His glory. When we undertake a challenge that is too great for us, and we accomplish that task *because* we have trusted God and God has moved in a miraculous way, God truly gets the credit. We must be quick to say, "I didn't do it. I could never have done it. God did it! He is the one who moved the mountains and made the way where there was no way. He deserves all praise, honor, and glory for this."

God wants to release you from heavy burdens, but He will not release you from a call He has placed on your life. Ask the Lord to reveal to you the difference between a burden that He does not desire for you to carry alone, or perhaps at all, and a call that He does desire you to pursue and will help you fulfill.

The Great Need for God's Wisdom

Ezra and his traveling companions needed protection for their journey, but first and foremost, they needed God's wisdom about how they were to travel. Every person faces the challenge of knowing how he should live. We have different needs at different times. We have different responsibilities, different relationships with our loved ones and family members, and different tasks to do at different times. Most of us know that we should keep the commandments of God and live in accordance with God's Word. However, the application of God's Word to any given situation, circumstance, environment, or relationship is usually a matter of knowing how to respond and make the right choices.

God's wisdom unfolds as we ask God for it. Rarely does God

give us a full plan for our lives from start to finish. We receive guidance moment by moment and day by day from the Holy Spirit. We need to be quick to ask for God's wisdom in any and every situation and to ask for it daily. A time of prayer and fasting for God's wisdom usually comes at times when we are facing a major challenge, opportunity, or decision, and we know that our lives will take on a very distinct quality depending on the decisions we make.

Very specifically, we need God's wisdom on:

- What to do—both what we need to let go of and what we need to take on.
- With whom we should be in relationships to get a task accomplished—and how to involve others or ask others to help us.
- How to proceed—practically, materially, financially.
- When to act and when to wait—and good use of time along the way.
- Where we should go.
- How we should organize the workload and responsibilities.

PREPARING FOR THIS FAST

The way we must come to a time of praying and fasting when we are burdened is this:

First, we need to acknowledge that we need help—we need a plan for addressing the burdens we have. We need to recognize that we cannot carry the full load by ourselves.

Second, we must ask God for His wisdom, fully believing the truth of James 1:5, which says, "If any of you lack wisdom, let him ask of God, that giveth to all men liberally, and upbraideth not; and it shall be given him." God promises to give us all of the knowledge, understanding, and wisdom we need . . .

and more. He never criticizes us or rejects us when we ask for His wisdom.

Third, we must be willing to lay down the burden at the feet of Jesus and pick up only that part of the burden that the Lord directs us to take. In giving up all of the burden to the Lord, we are saying, "Lord, I cannot carry this. Show me if there's any part of this that You want for me—any aspect of this that should remain my responsibility, be under my authority, be part of my workload, be part of my daily tasks and chores. And if there is a part of this load that I'm to continue to carry, help me to lift that load and carry it with a gracious and loving spirit."

Fourth, we must be quick to say to the Lord:

- "In areas where I cannot . . . You can."
- "In areas where I don't know what to do . . . You know."
- "In areas where I am limited . . . You are unlimited."
- "I trust You to help me do all I can do, and then I trust You to do what only You can do."

Anticipating the Devil's Lies

Be prepared for the devil's counterattack. The devil is likely to come to you during the beginning stage of your fast and tell you his pack of lies about your abilities and your burden:

- "You deserve this burden. You created the situation, you must bear the burden of it."
- "You have no right to ask for anybody's help, much less God's help."
- "You're a wimp. You can do this. You are giving up too easily."
- "You aren't under any more pressure than anybody else—do what you have to do."
- "What does God care about this burden of yours? He's got bigger things to deal with and more important people to help."

Lies, lies, and more lies! The devil is always a liar. Tell him so and begin to voice your trust in the Lord. God does care and He does want to help you.

PRAYING FOR GOD'S PLANS TO BE REVEALED

The Bible contains many verses about God's wisdom and His desire for His people to walk in understanding. Here are just a few you may want to use as the biblical foundation for your prayers in a time of fasting as you believe God to undo the heavy burden in your life:

- Cast thy burden upon the LORD, and he shall sustain thee: he shall never suffer the righteous to be moved. (Psalm 55:22)
- And it shall come to pass in that day, that his burden shall be taken away from off thy shoulder, and his yoke from off thy neck, and the yoke shall be destroyed because of the anointing. (Isaiah 10:27)
- He that trustest in his own heart is a fool: but whoso walketh wisely, he shall be delivered. (Proverbs 28:26)
- Behold, thou desirest truth in the inward parts: and in the hidden part thou shalt make me to know wisdom. (Psalm 51:6)
- If thou wilt receive my words, and hide my commandments with thee; so that thou incline thine ear unto wisdom, and apply thine heart to understanding; yea, if thou criest after knowledge, and liftest up thy voice for understanding; if thou seekest her as silver, and searchest for her as for hid treasures; then shalt thou understand the fear of the LORD, and find the knowledge of God. For the LORD giveth wisdom: out of his mouth cometh knowledge and understanding. He layeth up sound wisdom for the righteous: he is a buckler to them that walk uprightly. He keepeth the paths of

judgment, and preserveth the way of his saints. Then shalt thou understand righteousness, and judgment, and equity; yea, every good path. (Proverbs 2:1–9)

Praise and Thanksgiving for God's Plans

As you seek the divine plans that will release you from a heavy burden, praise God that His plans always are for your good. Remind yourself of Jeremiah 29:11—"For I know the thoughts that I think toward you, saith the LORD, thoughts of peace, and not of evil, to give you an expected end." Praise God that He is the giver of all gifts, the one who calls people into His service, and the one who has created all things. Praise God that He is the one who sees the beginning from the ending and has made a way for you to walk that is good in His sight.

- "I thank You, Lord, that You have guided my life to this point. I trust You to lead me forward in ways that honor You and bring glory to Your name."
- "I praise You, Lord, that You are the one who calls me to be successful and who enables me to be successful according to Your plans for me."
- "I thank You, Lord, that You love my friend [or family member] and want to help that person. If You have a plan for me to be of greater assistance or to share Your Word with this person, I thank You in advance for revealing that plan to me."
- "I thank You, Lord, that You are in complete charge of all things and that You never lead us into paths that are not well ordered."

Praying Specifically for Guidance

The Bible tells us, "Righteousness shall go before him; and shall set us in the way of his steps" (Ps. 85:13). It also says, "The steps of a good man are ordered by the LORD: and he delighteth in his way" (Ps. 37:23). As you pray for God's guidance, ask the

Lord specifically to order your steps. Ask Him to show you what to do first. And as you take that step, ask the Lord what to do next.

The Lord's leading is step by step and day by day. What God does promise to us is that when we pursue righteousness—when we seek to do those things that are right in God's eyes—He will guide us along a path that gives us delight. We will take pleasure in living out the plan God gives us. We won't feel burdened. We'll have joy!

Ask the Lord to lead you so clearly that you can hardly wait to get up the next morning to see what He has for you that day! Ask Him to restore your joy in caring for others, in doing the mundane daily tasks that you have to do, and in following the disciplines that cause you to grow spiritually, to experience greater physical and emotional health, and to stay alive mentally.

Ask the Lord to show you very plainly what He would have you do right now to begin to turn a burden into a blessing.

10

LETTING THE OPPRESSED GO FREE

Not long ago I heard about a person who lived in a very difficult place and under very trying circumstances. This person, however, did not feel at all oppressed. Rather, he felt excited that the Lord had put him into a position where he could be of great service and have a very effective soul-winning ministry.

I also heard about a woman who was in prison, a place most people would find oppressive. She knew that she had broken the law and deserved the punishment she received, but she also rejoiced because it was in prison that she heard about Jesus and accepted Him as her Savior. She then had a ministry of leading a Bible study and prayer group for other women in the prison with her. She did not feel at all oppressed.

Oppression is what a person feels when trapped in a situation in which he cannot see a purpose or a way out. Oppression is very closely linked to feelings of depression, hopelessness, and despair. It is often rooted in doubt. Those who are oppressed often are filled with fear, have very little joy, and they struggle to use their faith—they often are so oppressed they cannot even fathom a joyous day without fear or fathom the truth that they have a measure of faith to use against fear and doubt (Rom. 12:3).

Oppression has very little to do with the actual circumstance in which we may find ourselves. It has a great deal to do with how we perceive, feel, and respond to a circumstance or situation. You have a choice when it comes to how you evaluate and what you decide. Nothing forces you to feel oppressed or depressed—or to feel fear, worry, or doubt. Your emotions and your ability to believe are subject to your will, which God has given you in order that you might make choices that include Him and exclude the devil.

Sometimes people who aren't trapped still feel trapped! Other people feel very free even when they are in what other people see as horrible circumstances. The apostle Paul wrote a number of the books we have in the New Testament while he was in prison, including his letter to the Philippians. Read that book again and notice how many times Paul referred to joy, confidence, and peace—hardly the emotions that most people would expect from someone in a Roman prison! Oppression isn't about what is external to your life; it's about how you respond to life.

The way out of oppression is actually very simple to understand, but sometimes very difficult to do. It involves believing that God is in control of all things and that God desires all things to work for our eternal good. In other words, God is at work at all times and through all experiences to do a work in us that is for our benefit, now and forever.

SAMUEL'S FAST IN A TIME OF OPPRESSION

Samuel was not only the high priest of Israel after Eli, but he was also a judge of Israel. God used him to intercede for as well as to lead God's people in confronting and overcoming their enemies. During the time of Samuel, the Philistines repeatedly attacked the Israelites. In one of the battles between the Israelites and the

Philistines, the ark of the covenant was taken into captivity. Eventually, through a series of divine interventions, the ark was brought to the house of a man named Abinadab in a place called Kirjath-jearim. At that time, the Bible tells us, "all the house of Israel lamented after the LORD" (1 Sam. 7:2).

Samuel spoke to the Israelites, saying: "If ye do return unto the LORD with all your hearts, then put away the strange gods and Ashtaroth from among you, and prepare your hearts unto the LORD, and serve him only: and he will deliver you out of the hand of the Philistines" (1 Sam. 7:3).

The children of Israel did as Samuel had said. They began to serve only the Lord. Then Samuel called the leaders of Israel to a time of prayer and fasting. The Bible tells us: "They gathered together to Mizpeh, and drew water, and poured it out before the LORD, and fasted on that day, and said there, We have sinned against the LORD" (1 Sam. 7:6).

Mizpeh was the place in which the people were accustomed to coming to experience the presence of the Lord (Judg. 10:17, 11:11, 20:3, 21:5). Spies from the Philistines apparently knew that the leaders of the people had gathered there and they saw it as an opportune time to attack Israel. The Bible says, "When the children of Israel heard it, they were afraid of the Philistines. And the children of Israel said to Samuel, Cease not to cry unto the LORD our God for us, that he will save us out of the hand of the Philistines." Samuel made a burnt offering to the Lord and cried out to God . . . and "the LORD heard him" (1 Sam. 7:7–9).

An amazing thing happened. The Lord caused great thunder to come upon the Philistines. The thunder so confused the Philistines that the men of Israel left Mizpeh and pursued them, driving them well to the south. We read in 1 Samuel 7:13 that "the Philistines were subdued, and they came no more into the coast of Israel: and the hand of the LORD was against the Philistines all the days of Samuel."

Overcoming Fear and Doubt

God challenges those who feel oppressed to face their doubts and fears. God wants His people to walk in faith and strength, boldly taking on the Lord's enemies and defeating them. A person who is filled with doubt and fear cannot successfully wage spiritual warfare because such a person does not believe that God will be victorious. The psalmist had these feelings. Read what he said about oppression:

> Attend unto me, and hear me: I mourn in my complaint, and make a noise; because of the voice of the enemy, because of the oppression of the wicked: for they cast iniquity upon me, and in wrath they hate me. My heart is sore pained within me: and the terrors of death are fallen upon me. Fearfulness and trembling are come upon me, and horror hath overwhelmed me. And I said, Oh that I had wings like a dove! For then would I fly away, and be at rest. (Psalm 55:2–6)

Like so many people who are oppressed, the person who wrote this psalm wanted to flee. He saw no way out of his problem. He felt trapped. By the end of this psalm, however, faith had risen up in the psalmist's heart. He said, "Cast thy burden upon the LORD, and he shall sustain thee: he shall never suffer the righteous to be moved. . . . I will trust in thee" (Ps. 55:22–23).

At the very heart of doubt and fear is a failure to see that God is in control of all things. The Lord was in control of the Philistines. He just needed for His people to believe that He was! The Lord desired for the Israelites to be free of Philistine attacks and the oppression of fear that stalked them year after year. God just needed His people to believe that He could set and keep them free!

Countless people today do not seem to believe that God is in control of all things, let alone in control of all situations in their personal lives. Just as importantly, they do not believe that God can help them gain control over their own thoughts and feelings. Many people are content to live with their fears and doubts. It never dawns on them to confront their fears—many of which manifest in worry and anxiety. It never dawns on them to seek God for answers that will erase their doubts.

Some people don't believe that Christians can or should be oppressed if they are walking with God. Christians, however, can get discouraged just like non-Christians. Christians can become depressed. They can have anxiety. Don't think that just because you are born again you will be automatically free of all fear and doubt. The key is this: don't settle for a life filled with fear and doubt!

When you find yourself feeling discouraged, go immediately to God in prayer. If the depression does not lift from your life, go to *prayer and fasting.* Get serious about seeking God to discover the reasons for your fears and doubts, and be open to what God speaks to your heart about what you are to believe and do. Then, ask God to fill you with courage to move beyond fears and doubts, including anxiety.

The truth of God is that He wants you to be free of the fears that paralyze you, that hold you back from doing God's will, or that keep you from living in the fullness of God's promises to you. The truth of God is that He wants you to know in whom you believe and what you believe so doubt does not hinder your witness for the Lord Jesus Christ.

PREPARING FOR THIS FAST

As you prepare for a time of prayer and fasting to confront oppression, set yourself to do these things:

First, come together with other believers, especially others who are strong, joyful, and victorious in their faith. In other words, get with leaders in your church who will believe with you for God to free you from fear, doubt, and the ever-present worries that keep you in oppression. Remember that Samuel called the people to come together. There are specific times when you need to be in fellowship with others as you fast and pray. You need to be with them as they joyfully praise God and express their faith. You need their encouragement!

Second, make a commitment to put away—to remove from your life—anything that is causing you to worry, doubt, or feel fear. If you don't know what might be contributing to your feelings of doubt and fear, ask the Lord to reveal it to you. The children of Israel were very aware of the Philistines as their oppressors. In order to pray against oppression, you need to understand what is contributing to oppression in your life.

One woman told me that as she began a time of fasting and prayer, the Lord told her to turn off her television set after six o'clock every night. She thought that was a little odd, so she asked a leader in her church about it. The Lord gave a word of wisdom to that leader, who said, "Do this! It's of the Lord. The Lord is speaking to you to turn off all those programs that are contributing to your fears." This woman had struggled for months with a feeling of great dread that something bad was going to happen to her or her children. She knew the instant the leader spoke to her that she had her answer from God and she no longer needed to fast.

For the next six weeks, this woman did not watch television after six o'clock in the evening. She later said, "I realized as never before that most of the programs that I had been watching in the evening depicted violence and crimes or talked about crimes and trials for crimes. Even the local evening news was often about various crimes that had been committed in my city. These programs were fueling my fears."

Even as this woman realized what was contributing to her fears, she also found in prayer that she had not been trusting God as she should for her safety and that of her family. She kept being reminded again and again of Bible passages in which God protected His people. She read these passages repeatedly and then made a decision to memorize about two dozen verses that directly spoke to God's power to protect, save, rescue, and defeat His enemies. She said, "Anytime I began to feel fear, I said to the Lord, 'You are my Protector. You are my Fortress. You are the one who keeps me and my family from harm.'"

This woman was not only confronting her fears, she was also building up her faith. The oppression did not lift immediately from her life, but within a few weeks, she felt it go completely and it has never returned.

By the way, this woman never did return to a habit of watching secular television programs after six o'clock in the evening. She said, "I tune in only Christian programs, and I watch videos that teach God's Word and show praise gatherings. I am feeding my mind and my spirit the right food for faith."

I like that phrase: "the right food for faith." When we fill our minds with those things that strengthen our faith and that answer our doubts, we will be set free from fears and worries. Oppression will go!

Third, make a decision that you are going to trust God in a new way. Trust is a decision of your will: you can decide whether you are going to trust God to be in control of all things, or you are going to trust something or someone other than God. One of the greatest reasons to fast and pray is to seek a new level of trust in the Lord.

Fourth, focus on the purpose that God has for your life. When you begin to see that God has put you in a particular circumstance or situation—perhaps in a certain family or place of employment—for divine reasons, you will have a new purpose for your life. You will be able to overcome many doubts and fears as you see how God desires to use you in the lives of other people to lead them to Christ Jesus, establish righteousness in a particular neighborhood or environment, or bring healing and wholeness to those in need. It is no accident that you are where you are!

God had a tremendous purpose in having His people in the promised land, in having them overcome their enemies, including the Philistines. Part of that purpose was to encourage us, we who read the Bible today. Our faith is strengthened as we read how Samuel cried out to God and God answered him, and as we read how the children of Israel pursued the Philistines and subdued them. The ways you act in the midst of oppressing circumstances and situations will be a witness to others that may extend for many generations. Begin to see that God is giving you an opportunity to be strengthened in your faith so you might, in turn, help strengthen the faith of others.

Anticipating the Devil's Lies

As you begin to fast and pray, the enemy is likely to come with his lies to discourage you even further and create even more fear or doubt. He seems to come especially when a person begins a fast and is likely to feel a little low on energy. Among his lies are likely to be statements such as these:

- "Your family has a history of feeling depressed and discouraged [or a history of being worriers]. You are just made this way."
- "You have every reason to be afraid or doubtful. God must not love you to allow you to be in this very fearful and shaky situation."
- "You have to learn to cope. You can't truly be delivered from oppression."
- "Everybody has fears and doubts. This world is a scary place and nothing is sure."
- "Your enemies are stronger than you are. You'll never be set free from them."

Lies, lies, and more lies! Refuse to listen to them! Get into God's Word and quote the Bible back to the devil. Remind the devil what a good and great God you serve, and that He is the one in whom you are putting your trust.

PRAYING FOR RELEASE FROM OPPRESSION

The Bible has scores of verses and passages that speak about the strength of God to set captives free and to protect God's people. Here are just a few to help you get started as you fast and pray for freedom from oppression:

- The LORD hath done great things for us; whereof we are glad. Turn again our captivity, O LORD, as the streams in the south. They that sow in tears shall reap in joy. (Psalm 126:3–5)
- Ye shall seek me, and find me, when ye shall search for me with all your heart. And I will be found of you, saith the LORD: and I will turn away your captivity. (Jeremiah 29:13–14)
- Deliver me from the oppression of man: so will I keep thy precepts. (Psalm 119:134)
- O LORD, I am oppressed; undertake for me. (Isaiah 38:14)
- They that trust in the LORD shall be as mount Zion which cannot be removed, but abideth for ever. (Psalm 125:1)
- I called upon the LORD in distress: the Lord answered me, and set me in a large place. The LORD is on my side; I will not fear: what can man do unto me? The LORD taketh my part with them that help me: therefore shall I see my desire upon them that hate me. It is better to trust in the LORD than to put confidence in man. It is better to trust in the LORD than to put confidence in princes. (Psalm 118:5–9)
- As for God, his way is perfect: the word of the LORD is tried: he is a buckler to all those that trust in him. For who is God save the LORD? Or who is a rock save our God? It is God that girdeth me with strength, and maketh my way perfect. (Psalm 18:30–32)

Praise and Thanksgiving for Strength and Purpose

As you pray in your time of fasting, be sure to offer praise and thanksgiving in abundance. One of the keys to overcoming fear and doubt is praise. Praise God for:

- The Holy Spirit's being the Spirit of truth, the Comforter, the Counselor.
- His strong right arm that delivers His people from all oppression.
- Being in control of all things—all people, all situations, all circumstances.
- His desire to free you from oppression, depression, discouragement, and despair.
- His power to defeat every force of evil that comes against your life to discourage you, fill you with fear, or cause you to worry.
- His Word—the Bible—that builds your faith.

Also praise God for being your:

- Fortress—your place of protection.
- Rock—the foundation on which you build your entire life.
- Shield—the impenetrable protection against the fiery darts of fear and worry that the enemy of your spirit may launch against you.

There are countless things for which to thank the Lord:

- "Heavenly Father, I thank You for showing Yourself strong in my life." List before the Lord the many times in which He has protected you, provided for you, and helped you to overcome fear or depression.
- "Heavenly Father, I thank You for leading me to a time of trusting You in deeper and greater ways. I know You are

preparing me and teaching me how to trust You, and I am grateful."

- "Heavenly Father, I thank You in advance for setting me free from all things and all people that might be considered oppressors."

Praying Specifically for Freedom from Oppression

Ask the Lord specifically and directly to set you free. Only God knows the full story about how you developed feelings of oppression. Ask God to deal with anything and everything that led to your discouragement, depression, or oppression.

Ask the Lord to show you something that He may desire for you to do to separate yourself from a person or a situation that tends to foster doubt or fear in you. Ask the Lord to show you in very specific ways that He truly is in control of every area and every minute of your life.

If you feel low in your ability to trust God, ask God to help you trust Him more. A woman once said to a pastor, "I don't have faith."

The pastor replied, "Do you want to have more faith?"

The woman said, "No, not really."

The pastor said, "Do you *want* to want to have more faith?"

At this the woman smiled and said, "I can see where you're going, pastor. Yes, I want to want to have more faith."

The pastor said, "Then start with that. Admit to the Lord that you don't have faith but that you *want* to want to have more faith. God will meet you there."

Ask the Lord to increase your understanding of His love and care for you. I have no doubt that as you catch a glimpse of His vast love and His abundant care, you will have greater faith to trust Him to protect you and free you from all oppression.

11

BREAKING EVERY YOKE

We've talked about the fact that a yoke was a device placed across the shoulders of an animal to force that animal to do the bidding of a person who was in authority over it. At times, yokes were also placed across the shoulders of a prisoner, as in the case of Samson when the Philistines captured him and forced him to grind grain.

Not all yokes are bad. Jesus said, "Take my yoke upon you, and learn of me; for I am meek and lowly in heart: and ye shall find rest unto your souls. For my yoke is easy, and my burden is light" (Matt. 11:29–30).

The yoke of Jesus makes us productive for God's kingdom in a way that gives us purpose, deep feelings of satisfaction, and an abiding joy. Sometimes in my ministry I am weary in my body from travel, especially international trips. Even so, I always have a deep awareness that God has led me to a place for His purposes. I have seen God's hand at work. I come away from times of ministry tired, but at the same time, feeling fulfilled and joyful.

Have I been under a yoke? Yes.

Was the task difficult? Yes.

But did I find the completion of the task fulfilling? Absolutely!

The yoke of Jesus is "easy" because it fits us. It fits the new nature that we have after we are born again. It fits our talents and abilities. It fits the call of God on our lives. We can always rest assured that God does not call His people to fail. He calls us to succeed at life.

God gives us gifts . . . and shows us how to develop them and use them.

God gives us opportunities . . . and shows us how to pursue them.

God opens doors of service and ministry before us . . . and shows us how to walk through those doors.

God always leads us to use the gifts He has given to us, not the gifts we don't have. He always leads us to walk a path that He has designed for us, not the path He has prepared for someone else. He always leads us to be more conformed to the character of Christ Jesus. The work that God gives us to do gives us pleasure because He designed us to do that work.

The same is true for worship. The Lord yokes us to other believers so that our worship establishes God's presence on the earth in a way that attracts unbelievers and brings us great joy at the same time.

It is for these very reasons—work and worship—that we need to be very cautious about whom we become yoked up with. The Bible tells us very plainly, "Be not unequally yoked together with unbelievers: for what fellowship hath righteousness with unrighteousness? And what communion hath light with darkness? And what concord hath Christ with Belial? Or what part hath he that believeth with an infidel?" (2 Cor. 6:14–15).

The Bible also says: "Stand fast therefore in the liberty wherewith Christ hath made us free, and be not entangled again with the yoke of bondage" (Gal. 5:1). The apostle Paul was specifically addressing false doctrines that put heavy weights on people to keep various aspects of the law of Moses that Jesus had fulfilled by His death and resurrection. We must not allow ourselves to be put under the yoke of false teachers who assign people very strict rules and regimens that are contrary to the freedom Christ Jesus gives us.

THE FAST OF JONATHAN

One of the least-recognized fasts in the Bible is one Jonathan, the son of King Saul, kept. It lasted only a few select meals. It was a fast nonetheless. David may also have participated in this fast—we don't know. What we do know is that both Jonathan and David refused to keep a feast time in the way King Saul had prescribed it for them. We also know that both Jonathan and David were freed from the yokes Saul had put upon them.

At the time this fast occurred, Saul had made several threats against David's life. David knew that Saul was seeking to kill him out of jealousy at David's popularity, and even more importantly, out of fear at David's anointing by the Lord. Nevertheless, David was in the inner circle of the king's court. He was yoked to King Saul.

Jonathan, of course, was Saul's son and was yoked to his father as well.

The day came when David ran for his life from Saul. He met with Jonathan secretly and said, "There is but a step between me and death." Jonathan replied, "Whatsoever thy soul desireth, I will even do it for thee" (1 Sam. 20:3–4).

In saying this, Jonathan was taking the first step in breaking his yoke with his father. David and Jonathan then made a plan designed to show David whether Saul was still seeking to take his life. Jonathan and David made a covenant with each other—in essence, putting themselves under the same yoke to do the will of God in each other's lives, regardless of what King Saul might say or do (see 1 Sam. 20:5, 16).

The next day was the start of a special feasting time associated with the new moon. The Bible says, "The king sat him down to eat meat. And the king sat upon his seat, as at other times, even upon a seat by the wall: and Jonathan arose, and Abner sat by Saul's side, and David's place was empty" (1 Sam. 20:24–25). Normally King Saul, Abner, Jonathan, and David sat down and ate these feast meals together. On this day, Jonathan arose—he came to the table, but he rose before he ate. David was absent. King Saul didn't seem to notice that anything was different.

But on the second day of the feast time, King Saul was very aware that David's place was empty. He asked his son about David's absence, and when Jonathan told him that David was away celebrating the feast with his father, he recognized that Jonathan had put himself in an alliance with David. He was so angry he threw a javelin at Jonathan—he tried to kill his own son and desired heir. The Bible says, "So Jonathan arose from the table . . . and did eat no meat the second day of the month: for he was grieved for David, because his father had done him shame" (1 Sam. 20:34).

There are times when we need to refuse to sit down to business as usual. Instead, we need to rise up and make a change.

The following morning, Jonathan went into a field according to the prearranged plan with David. There, Jonathan shot arrows beyond a target and shouted at his servant who went to find them, "Is not the arrow beyond thee?" (1 Sam. 20:37). In his hiding place, David received this message loud and clear. He knew that it was not safe to return to King Saul's court. In fact, it would never be safe for him to return to the presence of King Saul.

The yoke that tied David into an alliance with Saul was broken that day. In significant ways, the yoke that tied Jonathan to the throne of Israel and to his father was also definitively broken that day. David and Jonathan wept together that they would no longer be in close friendship, and then Jonathan said to David,

"Go in peace, forasmuch as we have sworn both of us in the name of the LORD, saying, The LORD be between me and thee, and between my seed and thy seed for ever" (1 Sam. 20:42).

Was David still under God's anointing to be king of Israel one day? Absolutely.

Was David allowed to prepare to become king in what many would see as the logical place of preparation, the king's court? No.

Was David set free from the yoke of being part of King Saul's close inner circle? Yes.

Was this difficult? Very. It meant that David would spend the next years of his life on the run, often hiding out in caves. It meant that David would face challenges and situations he had never dreamed of facing. But did this yoke need to be broken so that David could grow in his trust of the Lord and in his understanding about how to lead men into peace and not just into battle? Yes!

Judging the Situation

When people encounter work-related obstacles to righteousness, they often face the question *Am I being judgmental?* We are to be people of judgment when it comes to recognizing what is good and evil (see 1 Pet. 4:17). Yet Jesus also commanded us, "Judge not, and ye shall not be judged" (Luke 6:37). Jesus was referring to our judgment of people. Judgment, of course, includes determining a person's innocent or guilt before God, and on the basis of our decision, passing a sentence on what should happen to a person. Jesus said we are in no position to know the whole story about any person, including his motives or intents. We are to judge whether something is sinful but not pass sentence on sinners.

When we are evaluating a work relationship, we are wise to recognize that something is wrong when it comes to values and abuses. We are never right in condemning another person to our coworkers or being in rebellion to a superior. David is a good example to us in this. David fled from the court of King Saul. He clearly recognized that the way Saul was treating him was wrong. He knew his life was in danger and that Saul was acting in an ungodly way. But David never did anything to undermine the reputation or the reign of King Saul. He always defended Saul's right to be king and he refused to say anything against him.

Jonathan, too, cast his lot with David. He knew that David would be king. He honored God's anointing on David's life. But he did not rebel against his father or seek to take the throne from him. We have no mention that Jonathan ever said anything against Saul to the other people in King Saul's court.

The Alliances That Yoke Us

Every person today is allied with someone for the purpose of getting a task accomplished. That alliance may be in a job. It may be in a club or on a committee. It may be in a church or ministry. Anytime we are in an alliance that involves our time and talent to accomplish a given mission or job we are, in many ways, under a yoke. We are bound with other people to get something done. We must be very sure that God has put us into this alliance. We must be very sure that God desires for us to get a particular task done with the people who are yoked to our lives.

I can't begin to tell you how many people I know who do or endure certain things because they believe the ends justify the means. They see a project or a job as being worthy, and at times even necessary. In their desire to see the job accomplished, they put up with all kinds of things that may be wrong, even sinful. They seem to think that as long as they reach the end goal, the way of reaching the goal will cease to be important before the Lord. The truth is that God is as concerned with how you reach a goal, and with whom you work, as He is with the goal that you pursue.

Now I'm not at all referring to personality differences or to different preferences when it comes to style or methodology. I'm referring to people compromising their values, keeping quiet about their faith in Jesus, or putting up with repeated abusive behavior in order to keep their jobs, keep on track with a project, or keep a club membership.

There are times when God requires us to stand up and say, "No more. I will not be party to this. I will not be yoked to this project [or this employer, this group, this goal] if it means that I must compromise my relationship with Jesus Christ."

Let me give you an example. I heard recently about a man who went on an international business trip for his corporation. The purpose of the trip—which was scheduled to last ninety days—was to develop specific plans for helping the people in a foreign nation to dig new water wells and harness solar power for electricity to outlying areas. The company saw this as a good humanitarian gesture, but also as a way of expanding its business in this region. This particular man, whom I will call Tom, was glad to be part of a corporation that had a concern for poor people in other nations. He went on the trip with two other men from different branch offices.

As they traveled to this foreign land, Tom quickly discovered that the other two men were not Christians and were very sinful in their behavior. Nevertheless, Tom agreed to share a three-bedroom apartment with them in the city where they would be working overseas. Tom's traveling companions suggested this as a way of saving money for the corporation, although Tom later learned that they intended to invoice the corporation for three one-bedroom apartments and personally pocket the difference. The men also told Tom that they thought sharing an apartment was good for their personal safety. Since Tom had never been to the city or nation before and the other two men had several times, he agreed to the plan.

Tom was not at all prepared, however, for the nightly appearance of prostitutes at the doorstep of their apartment! The other two men routinely invited these women into their bedrooms. Tom was appalled, but he remained quiet . . . and miserable. Finally Tom confronted the other two men and said, "I need to get a place of my own." He told them how wrong he thought it was to steal corporation money and to engage in prostitution. The other men threatened him, saying that if he moved out or told people back in the United States how they behaved overseas, they would trump up accusations against him that would cause him to be fired.

Tom knew that both of the men had friends high in the corporation. He had no doubt they could make good on their threats. Tom didn't know what to do—which is a very good time, of course, to pray and fast! Tom began to devote his noon meal each day to fasting and praying. This, interestingly, is the meal that Jonathan fasted.

Over the course of the next two weeks of praying and fasting, Tom realized that he felt himself yoked with unbelievers. He knew he had to move out, regardless of any threats made against him . . . and he did.

As soon as Tom returned to the United States, he offered a letter of resignation. Tom knew that he could not be under the yoke of a corporation that would allow behavior like this among its top personnel. He certainly could not be under the yoke of working with these two men on this project in the coming months, nor could he work with them on any future projects. In his exit interview, Tom was asked why he was resigning and he was very candid in expressing the reasons for his departure. The man conducting the interview seemed upset, but he also said that his hands were tied. He couldn't do anything on Tom's behalf. Tom moved on to another job.

Nearly three years later, Tom learned that both of these men had contracted HIV, very likely from prostitutes overseas. They were very sick. The corporate project had stalled. Key people higher up in the corporation had resigned. Tom called his former supervisor to express his sadness at the way things had turned out, and in the end, the corporation hired Tom back with a clear understanding about what Tom would and would not do.

After the yoke of this alliance was broken from Tom's life, he grew greatly in his faith. When he returned to the corporation, he found that he was in a position to have a much stronger witness for the Lord. Several people who knew the stand he had taken told him how much they respected what he had done. Within several months, Tom led several of his coworkers to the Lord.

PREPARING FOR THIS FAST

As you prepare to enter a time of fasting and praying about a particular yoke in your life, there are certain things you must do:

First, focus on those relationships in your life that are work- or task-related. Family relationships—such as that between a parent and a child or between spouses—are yoked relationships, but we will cover those in another chapter. This is a time to focus on yokes that cause us to plow or cultivate a field under the authority of another person or in alliance with other people.

Second, focus on any issues related to values, character, or your witness for the Lord. Let personality differences and petty disagreements over procedures go by the wayside. These issues may be troublesome to you, but they are not likely reasons that determine whether you will stay in or leave a relationship.

Third, recognize that, in fasting and praying about the yokes of your life, you are calling all of your work-related relationships into question before the Lord. Be open to ways in which the Lord shows you how to be a better witness or how to stand up for what is right in God's eyes.

Also be open to ways in which the Lord may reveal to you the compromising you are doing when it comes to your values or beliefs. Many times we are not aware that we are compromising—we think we are simply keeping quiet. The Lord may show you that in keeping quiet, you are failing to speak what He desires you to speak.

The Lord may also show you that you are being obnoxious or that you are doing things that cause others to persecute you. You may be the reason for some of the friction and disagreement you feel in your place of work or committee meetings. Be open to asking the Lord to reveal to you all ways in which you may not be yoked up appropriately, as well as ways in which you may be fighting against the work God has put before you.

Anticipating the Devil's Lies

Recognize that the devil is likely to come to you with lies related to a specific yoke you are under:

- "The ends *do* justify the means."
- "If you quit, the job won't get done."
- "If you quit this alliance [or partnership or membership], people will call you a quitter and you'll get a bad reputation."
- "You have to compromise on values sometimes in order to make friends with people so you can lead them to the Lord."

Lies, lies, and more lies! Simply refuse to listen to them.

PRAYING FOR GOD TO BREAK THE YOKE OF BONDAGE

As you search God's Word during your time of fasting and praying, use a concordance to find references that relate to standing strong in the face of what is wrong. For example:

- Stand not in an evil thing. (Ecclesiastes 8:3)
- Blessed is the man that walketh not in the counsel of the ungodly, nor standeth in the way of sinners, nor sitteth in the

seat of the scornful. But his delight is in the law of the LORD; and in his law doth he meditate day and night. And he shall be like a tree planted by the rivers of water, that bringeth forth his fruit in his season; his leaf also shall not wither; and whatsoever he doeth shall prosper. The ungodly are not so: but are like the chaff which the wind driveth away. Therefore the ungodly shall not stand in the judgment, nor sinners in the congregation of the righteous. For the LORD knoweth the way of the righteous: but the way of the ungodly shall perish. (Psalm 1)

- My son, if sinners entice thee, consent thou not. . . . My son, walk not thou in the way with them; refrain thy foot from their path: for their feet run to evil, and make haste to shed blood. (Proverbs 1:10, 15–16)

I especially encourage you to read the book of Proverbs as you fast and pray to break a yoke over your life. Much of this book is related to what it means to avoid alliances with those who pursue unrighteous goals or act in unrighteous ways.

Praise and Thanksgiving to Release a Yoke of Bondage

In many ways, offering thanksgiving and praise breaks the emotional hold that a situation might have over you. It is in praise and thanksgiving that we often gain the courage and strength to confront those who are abusing us or attempting to control our work situations in unrighteous ways. Thank the Lord for His presence with you and praise Him for calling you out of sin and to a closer walk with the Lord.

- "Thank You, Heavenly Father, for bringing godly people into my life to support me, teach me, mentor me, disciple me, and help me."
- "Thank You, Heavenly Father, for the many times in which You have not only showed me what You wanted me to do

but how to accomplish Your goals and act in Your timing." Be specific in your thanksgiving for God's guidance at very specific times and in very specific situations.

- "Thank You, Heavenly Father, for guarding my heart when I have been yoked with unrighteous people and for helping me to break those associations." Again, be specific about ways in which the Lord has helped you in the past.

Praise the Lord for the many ways in which He says in His Word that He will be your:

- Companion.
- Husband (to the widow) or Father (to the orphan).
- Guide or Counselor.
- Helper—of yourself and the one called alongside to help.

Praise the Lord for being the *Lord* of your life. Lordship speaks directly to the issue of work and to relationships. A lord tells his servants what to do and with whom. A lord puts his servants together in yoked relationships to accomplish specific tasks. A lord tells his servants when to act and how. When we declare and praise Jesus as Lord of our lives, we are saying to Him, "You are my Master. Order my work. Order my relationships. Order my time."

Praying Specifically for the Right Yokes

We all are in alliance or association with other people in the course of our lives. We tend to have a number of relationships that are geared to accomplishing goals and doing tasks. Pray specifically for God to send His chosen people into your life to help you. Pray that God will send you to specific people to help them.

Use your time of fasting and prayer to focus on the alliances that the Lord wants you to make in your life. Seek His counsel about how you are to pursue the goals He sets before you and with whom you are to pursue godly goals.

PRAYING AND FASTING
FOR WHOLENESS

Five of the main purposes to fast in Isaiah 58 are related to wholeness in a person's life. Although the prophet's words are aimed at the entire body of God's people, his words certainly may be applied to the individual or family:

- Feeding the hungry.
- Providing for the poor.
- Clothing the naked.
- Restoring family relationships.
- Bringing healing speedily.

Each of these reasons to fast and pray is aimed at moving us toward greater physical, emotional, and spiritual healing and wholeness.

Throughout His ministry, Jesus said to people, "Be thou made whole." Whenever anything was lacking or out of balance in a person's life, Jesus provided what was missing, restored what had been broken, or called a person back to the right priorities. There's an old saying that Jesus came to "take off you what the devil put on you, cast out of you what the devil put in you, create in you what God wants in you, and put on you what God desires for you to carry."

Jesus called people to pursue God's highest and best in their lives. He calls you and me to do the same.

Fasting puts us into an enhanced position to know what is missing, broken, damaged, or out of balance. Prayer puts us into a greater reliance upon the Lord to heal, restore, reconcile, balance, or create what we need for balance and wholeness.

Each of the needs addressed in this section is very practical. Certainly there are spiritual elements, but there also are down-to-earth, real-life dimensions to the needs represented in these fasts.

To encourage your faith, let me share with you an example in which a group of people prayed and fasted for God to meet a practical need related to their provision—indeed, to the preservation of their lives.

Many people think of the Pilgrims who came to North America on the *Mayflower* and landed at Plymouth Rock as old men and women wearing black clothing. The men are often shown with long, flowing, white beards. The majority of the Pilgrims, however, were young men and women. William Bradford, the governor of the colony, was thirty-one years old in 1621 when he took office. Most of the other Pilgrims were about the same age.

Unlike the Puritans, who sought reform within the traditional church in England, the Pilgrims were seeking liberty from old, unproductive forms of religion. They felt as if they were on a pilgrimage of truth. They believed the purpose of God was to restore the church to the way it was in New Testament times. They came to the New World from Nottinghamshire, Lincolnshire, and Yorkshire in England, seeking a new opportunity for worship.

Bradford wrote a book about life on Plymouth Plantation. He described the purpose for which the Pilgrims had come to North America: "[They] joined themselves (by a covenant of the laws) into a church estate, in the fellowship of the Gospel . . . for the propagating and advancing of the Gospel of the Kingdom of Christ in the remote parts of the world; yea though they should be but even as stepping stones unto others for the performing of so great a work."

Bradford described a public fast in the summer of 1623, a year in which the Pilgrims' corn crop was in trouble:

> By a great drought which continued from the third week in May, 'til about the middle of July without any rain and with great heat for the most part, insomuch as the corn began to wither away. It began to languish sore, and some of the drier grounds were parched like withered hay ... upon which we set apart a solemn day of humiliation to seek the Lord by humble and fervent prayer.
>
> ... And He was pleased to give gracious and speedy answer, both to their own and the Indians' admiration. ... For all the morning and the greatest part of the day, it was clear within and very hot, and not a cloud or any sign of rain to be seen; yet toward evening it began to overcast, and shortly after to rain with such sweet and gentle showers as gave them cause of rejoicing and blessing God.

Bradford went on to describe the results:

> It came without either wind or thunder or any violence, and by degrees in that abundance as that the earth was thoroughly ... soaked therewith. Which did so apparently revive and quicken the decayed corn and other fruits, as was wonderful to see, and made the Indians astonished to behold. And afterwards, the Lord sent them such seasonable showers, with interchange of fair warm weather as, through his blessing, caused a fruitful and liberal harvest.

Setting aside special days of fasting and prayer became an accepted part of life in Plymouth Colony. On November 15, 1636, a law was passed allowing the governor and his assistants "to command solemn days of humiliation by fasting, etc. And, also, for thanksgiving as occasion shall be offered."

The Lord desires us to trust Him completely when it comes to our needs in this earthly life. God desires to make us whole—body, soul, and spirit!

12

FEEDING THE HUNGRY

Each of us has a physical need for food. We also have a hunger for affection, attention, reward, satisfaction, and love. We have a hunger for God—every person feels, at some point in his or her life, a need to be in relationship with his or her Creator. A hunger might also be described as a drive, a motivating force, or a deep desire. We are hungry on many different levels of our lives, and God provides for us just the right food to meet our needs.

The Lord often leads us to prayer and fasting as a time for us to:

- *Address issues related to physical hunger.* A number of issues are related to physical hunger and food, most notably being overweight, being sick, and being anorexic or bulimic. A fast can help a person come to grips with eating too much or too little, having false beliefs about foods, and eating the wrong foods.
- *Address issues related to emotional hunger.* Every person has emotional needs to be valued, loved, appreciated, rewarded, and counted as worthy. I have had many years of experience praying for sick people and teaching people about God's principles of health. I have discovered along the way that deep emotional needs are often at the root of a physical

problem, a weight problem (either too much weight or too little), or an eating disorder. Resolving a long-standing emotional issue is often the key to resolving a physical problem associated with food.

WHEN HUNGER TURNS TO CRAVING

Since every person has a physical need for food and an emotional need for love and value, when do we need to become concerned about hunger? When it becomes a craving. A craving is an out-of-control desire.

Hunger becomes a craving when you can't say no to a certain food. Hunger is a craving when your first thought in the morning is about what you are going to eat during the day . . . when you find yourself planning your next snack or meal even as you are eating your current meal . . . and when your last thought at night is about what you are going to eat the next day.

Emotional hunger turns to a craving when you can't get enough attention or affection—when nothing a person says to you, does for you, or gives to you meets your need to be valued and appreciated. The person who is emotionally hungry wants more and more from another person or people—more time, more recognition, more reward, more expressions of touching and honoring.

How does fasting and prayer address cravings? The primary way to address an out-of-control physical or emotional craving is by turning those appetites into a spiritual hunger.

A spiritual hunger is rooted in a deep desire to know God more intimately and to know His Word more thoroughly. A spiritual hunger is born of a desire to draw closer to God and to be a more effective witness for the Lord on this earth.

Fasting and praying are the primary ways of turning a craving into a heart's new desire to know God's will and then do

God's will. We must seek to know God's will for every aspect of our hunger—especially our physical and emotional hungers. We must begin to trust God to meet our needs.

FASTING TO BE FED

It seems a great mystery to say that we fast from food in order to be fed in our spirits and souls. Nevertheless, the truth is this: anytime we want more of God, or more of God's help in any area of our lives, we are wise to fast and pray and allow God to feed us what we need for genuine eternal nourishment.

Over the years I have prayed for thousands of people to lose weight. One of the greatest healings I have ever seen was one a woman experienced during a season of fasting and prayer. She was in her twenties when she came for prayer. She told how a family friend had raped her when she was thirteen years old. She was so terrified of being raped again that she began to gain weight as a defense against being sexually attractive or sexually attacked. She wanted to make herself so undesirable to all men that they would leave her alone. Then, when she reached her twenties, she had a desire to marry. By that time she was grossly overweight.

After we prayed for this young woman, she had a dream in which she was walking down a dark path. The man who attacked her when she was thirteen years old stood before her, threatening her life. At that moment in her dream, Jesus appeared and the man fled. Then Jesus said to her, "Daughter, I have delivered you. From this moment you will lose weight." During the coming year, she lost 140 pounds!

I don't know what issues you may have with food and eating, but I do know this: God has a weight-loss plan that is just right for you. He will help you get to the right weight if you will trust Him to help you.

THE FAST OF ELIJAH AND A WIDOW IN ZAREPHATH

A fast that deals specifically with food, hunger, and eating is found in 1 Kings 17. The prophet Elijah had proclaimed the word of the Lord: "As the LORD God of Israel liveth, before whom I stand, there shall not be dew nor rain these years, but according to my word" (v. 1). Then the Lord sent Elijah into hiding by the Cherith brook.

There, the Lord fed Elijah with water from the brook and sent ravens to bring him food. The Bible tells us that the ravens brought Elijah bread and flesh in the morning, and bread and flesh in the evening (1 Kings 17:6). In many ways, this was a limited fast. Elijah received two meals a day—whatever amounts of bread and meat the birds dropped to him.

There certainly was not a great quantity of food.

There certainly was not a great variety of food.

Furthermore, Elijah had no control or influence whatsoever as to what he ate or precisely when. God provided what he needed to stay alive, but there can be little doubt that it wasn't everything that Elijah wanted.

After a while—we aren't told how long—the brook dried up and the Lord then said to Elijah, "Arise, get thee to Zarephath, which belongeth to Zidon, and dwell there: behold, I have commanded a widow woman there to sustain thee" (1 Kings 17:9).

Elijah did as he was told and when he reached Zarephath, he found the widow woman gathering sticks at the gate of the city. He asked her for a little water and when she brought it to him, he said, "Bring me, I pray thee, a morsel of bread in thine hand." She replied that she did not have anything like that to give. She told him that she had only a "handful of meal in a barrel, and a little oil in a cruse" (1 Kings 17:11–12). She explained that she was gathering sticks to make a fire so she might cook this last little bit of meal and oil into a cake for herself and her son.

Elijah told her to make him a little cake first, then afterward to make a cake for herself and her son. He said, "For thus saith the LORD God of Israel, The barrel of meal shall not waste, neither shall the cruse of oil fail, until the day that the LORD sendeth rain upon the earth." The woman believed the prophet and did as he said. The result was that "she, and he, and her house [her son], did eat many days. And the barrel of meal wasted not, neither did the cruse of oil fail, according to the word of the LORD, which he spake by Elijah" (1 Kings 17:14–16).

What is it that this widow, the prophet Elijah, and the widow's son ate for what may have been about a thousand meals? Small cakes made of whole-grain meal and a little olive oil!

Again, there certainly was not a great quantity of food.

There certainly was not a great variety of food.

Furthermore, neither Elijah, the widow, or the son had any control or influence whatsoever as to altering this meal plan. The nation was in a serious drought and famine—there were no food options.

PREPARING FOR THIS FAST

What does this story about Elijah and the widow in Zarephath say to us about fasting? How are we to prepare for a fast that addresses the issue of feeding the hungry?

First, we must ask God how much we are to eat—not just during our season of fasting and praying, but throughout the rest of our lives. Certainly because we are fasting, our food intake is likely to be far less or none at all. But what about our intake after we fast? We must be open to the great likelihood that God will direct us very specifically about the quantity of food we take into our bodies. For those who are overweight, He will likely command us to eat less; for those who are underweight or have an eating disorder, He is likely to command us to eat more (and refuse to purge after eating).

Second, we must ask God what we are to eat. If you do not

know which foods are best for health, become informed. I recommend that you seek out this information after you have ended your time of fasting, since focusing on foods during a fast can be counterproductive and discouraging. Rather, during the time of fasting and praying, ask the Lord to show you where to go and whom to consult about nutrition. (I wrote a book titled *Your Total Health Handbook* that may be of help to you. It covers all the basics of eating for a healthy body, soul, and spirit.)

Third, we must stick to all God's directions. During your season of fasting and praying, as the Lord reveals to you how much and what you should be eating, ask the Lord to help you address other issues related to your intake of food. Ask the Lord these questions:

- "How much exercise should I be doing? When in my schedule? How frequently?"
- "What types of exercise should I be doing?"
- "Should I continue a time of periodic fasting—perhaps fasting several meals a week or one day a week? Should I fast by limiting certain food groups?"
- "Are there emotional issues underlying my intake of food? What are they, and how can I be healed in my emotions?"
- "Are disease or metabolic issues underlying the problems I have with food? How can I be healed of them?"
- "What might I do to develop greater willpower in this area? In what ways do I need to rely upon the Holy Spirit more? How might I go about making a daily commitment to obeying You when it comes to my eating and exercising? Is there someone I need to ask for help? Is there someone to whom I need to be accountable in this?"

People who fast solely to lose weight often find that they regain even more weight after a fast. Although fasting can be a way to lose a few pounds, if you are seriously overweight (more than fifteen to twenty pounds), you need to do a modified fast and then pursue a weight-loss program. It is extremely important that you continue to lose weight in a healthful, slow manner, all the while increasing your exercise. (Before commencing a fast, you should assess your health and consider visiting a health professional.)

Fourth, specifically ask the Lord to give you a plan for living with optimal energy and strength. Appearance is never as important as health. God desires for you to have energy to do all the things He desires for you to accomplish. He desires for you to have persevering, enduring strength. He desires for you to be strong and flexible so you might avoid as many injuries as possible. Ask God for His total health plan!

Anticipating the Devil's Lies

Be aware that the devil will always come to you in a time of fasting to say, "You should be eating! You need food! You need your strength! It's wrong to deprive yourself of what you need!"

The devil often lies to us by giving us only part of the truth. It's true that we do need food and we do need strength. The whole truth, however, is that we generally do not need as much food as we eat. We nearly always do not need some of the foods we are eating—especially when it comes to substances that can harm our bodies.

The devil may also say:

- "You don't need to quit eating [your favorite food craving]. After all, you deserve a little pleasure!"
- "So what if you are overweight? It won't matter in the long run of your life."
- "It's nobody's business how you deal with food. It certainly isn't a spiritual matter."
- "Just rest. You're weak. You shouldn't exercise."
- "You have always been overweight [or underweight]. That's just the way you are. There's no use in trying to change."

Lies, lies, and more lies! Speak the truth to the devil. "Resist [him], and he will flee from you" (James 4:7).

PRAYING FOR GOD'S FEEDING

Rather than give you specific verses for this fast, I want to encourage you to read, meditate on, and study three passages of Scripture that refer to God's provision for hunger:

1. Read about how God provided manna for the children of Israel in the wilderness. (Exod. 16)
2. Read about how God chastised His people when they were not satisfied with what He provided. (Num. 11)
3. Read about God's promise to gather and provide for His people. (Ezek. 34:11–16)

As you read and study, ask the Lord to show you how to apply these passages to the physical provision of literal food, emotional provision for emotional hunger, and spiritual provision for spiritual hunger.

Praise and Thanksgiving in a Fast Aimed at Food Issues

While it seems obvious to praise and thank God for giving you food, I recommend that you focus your praise and thanksgiving in these areas:

- "Heavenly Father, I thank You for giving me the body I have. You made me with a specific body type, blood type, bone structure, height, and metabolism. You made me for health. Thank You that Your desire for me is always optimal health."
- "Thank You, Heavenly Father, for giving me a desire to come to grips with the food and eating issues in my life."

- "Thank You, Heavenly Father, for revealing Your total health plan to me as I fast and pray."
- "I praise You for being the Source of everything I need, including a strong and energetic body. I praise You for being my Healer, not only of my body but also of my emotions."

Praying Specifically for God's Health Plan

Ask the Lord very specifically to give you:

- Healing in your cardiovascular system—your heart, blood vessels, lungs, and blood.
- Healing in your bones, joints, skin, and muscles.
- Healing in your emotions and the way you think and feel about food, weight, exercise, and weight loss.
- Healing in your digestive organs.
- Healing in every aspect of your body—complete freedom from all allergies and infections.
- Healing in your metabolism and in the hormonal systems of your body.

Ask the Lord to give you greater immunity.

Ask the Lord to give you faith to believe for a total healing.

Ask the Lord to deliver you from food cravings and to instill in you a desire for foods that are healthy. Ask the Lord to instill in you a desire to exercise.

Ask the Lord for energy and strength.

13

PROVIDING FOR THE POOR AND CLOTHING THE NAKED

Every year in our church, a number of people enter a season of fasting and praying for material and financial needs. Some have a genuine lack of money or material goods in their lives. Some need to reset priorities when it comes to spending the resources God has put or is putting in their hands. Some need to trust God for additional income so they can meet specific needs in their lives or in the lives of others—including needs they desire to meet in suffering people around the world. The fast Isaiah proclaimed in Isaiah 58 includes "providing for the poor" and "clothing the naked." These are two expressions, I believe, of a broader concept: meeting material needs. Therefore, I am linking these two purposes for fasting together into one chapter.

PROVIDING FOR THE POOR

In Bible times people usually provided for the poor by lending items and providing work for people in need. Often the two were linked. A person or family might loan material items—including money, food, and goods—and then set up a work plan so that the poor person could earn what he needed to support himself and his family and pay back the loan. God gave a number of commandments for the way in which people were to handle this loan and work. For example:

- The creditor was to completely forgive the loan during the year of release, also called the Year of Jubilee. This came every seven years, and it was a time when all debts were canceled. Those who made loans were to make them freely, even if they knew the year of release was just months away.
- The creditor was to make the loan in a way that preserved the honor of the person receiving it.
- The work was never to be more burdensome than what the lender would be willing to do for the receiver.
- The creditor was to allow the borrower to work in a way that allowed the poor person to keep the Law of Moses regarding the Sabbath day and other restrictions related to being clean before the Lord.

Overall, however, "providing for the poor" was a phrase used to describe any type of honorable employment opportunity.

CLOTHING THE NAKED

"Clothing the naked" was a term often used in a more general way for gifts to the poor. At times, of course, this was giving money or material goods to meet a specific need in a person's life. At times it was just what the phrase states: giving tunics or cloaks, which people also used as blankets and as protection against inclement weather. Even in the time of Jesus, a woman named Tabitha (or Dorcas) was recognized for her good deeds in making garments and giving them to those in need (Acts 9:36).

People were to give gifts of any kind willingly, generously, and secretly. They were never to cause embarrassment to the person receiving the gift. The gifts were never to be a point of pride on the part of the giver.

Two of the key passages in the Bible that deal with these issues are:

1. Exodus 22:26–27: If thou at all take thy neighbour's raiment to pledge, thou shalt deliver it unto him by that the sun goeth down: for that is his covering only, it is his raiment for his skin: wherein shall he sleep? And it shall come to pass, when he crieth unto me, that I will hear; for I am gracious.

2. Deuteronomy 15:7–11: If there be among you a poor man of one of thy brethren within any of thy gates in thy land which the LORD thy God giveth thee, thou shalt not harden thine heart, nor shut thine hand from thy poor brother: but thou shalt open thine hand wide unto him, and shalt surely lend him sufficient for his need, in that which he wanteth.

   Beware that there be not a thought in thy wicked heart, saying, The seventh year, the year of release, is at hand; and thine eye be evil against thy poor brother, and thou givest him nought; and he cry unto the LORD against thee, and it be sin unto thee.

   Thou shalt surely give him, and thine heart shall not be grieved when thou givest unto him: because that for this thing the LORD thy God shall bless thee in all thy works, and in all that thou puttest thine hand unto.

   For the poor shall never cease out of thy land: therefore I command thee, saying, Thou shalt open thine hand wide unto thy brother, to thy poor, and to thy needy, in thy land.

THE FAST OF THE APOSTLE PAUL AND HIS SHIPMATES

Acts 27 is certainly one of the most exciting chapters in the Bible. This chapter deals with Paul's trip by sea from Caesarea to Rome. The trip took place in the fall, a time when sailing the Mediterranean could be quite dangerous. Paul, a prisoner of Rome, gave the crew a warning from the Lord that the trip would involve hurt and much damage, not only to the ship and its cargo but to human lives. Everyone ignored what Paul said. Not long after this, a terrible storm arose and over a period of two weeks, the crew threw most of the cargo and the rigging of the ship overboard to lighten the vessel so it might outrun the storm.

One night Paul received a word from the Lord, which he shared with others on board. God told him that the ship would be lost but all of their lives would be spared. They were to drive the ship toward a certain island, but even when they got fairly close to the island, they were not to jump overboard. Then Paul said,

> This day is the fourteenth day that ye have tarried and continued fasting, having taken nothing. Wherefore I pray you to take some meat: for this is for your health: for there shall not an hair fall from the head of any of you. And when he had thus spoken, he took bread, and gave thanks to God in presence of them all: and when he had broken it, he began to eat. Then were they all of good cheer, and they also took some meat. (Acts 27:33–36)

After they had eaten, they lightened the ship one more time, casting all the remaining wheat into the sea.

The following morning, they made a run for the shore. In the process, the ship ran aground and broke apart. All of the people made it safely to land just as Paul had said.

PREPARING FOR THIS FAST

What should we consider as we go into a time of fasting and praying for God's provision of material and financial resources?

First, we need to be open to guidance from the Lord as to what we are to give—as well as receive.

Second, we need to be open to the Lord's guidance regarding our employment. God may very well guide us into new positions or show us how to be more productive, creative, efficient, or effective in our work. One man told me not long ago that during a season of fasting and prayer the Lord had revealed to him what he needed to do to receive a promotion and a raise. He had followed the Lord's plan and within six months, he had received a new position that included a 50 percent increase in his take-home pay.

Let me point out to you three great truths from Paul's shipwreck that relate directly to God's provision—either directly through giving and receiving, or through working. Keep these truths at the forefront of your mind and heart as you enter a fast aimed at providing for the poor, clothing the naked, and meeting your material needs:

1. God gave very specific instructions about what the crew was to keep on board and what to throw overboard. As you pray and fast about material and financial issues in your life, seek God about what you need to give up and what you need to keep. There may be material items and property that you need to sell in order to pay off a debt or give the money toward the spreading of the gospel. Be open to whatever God tells you to "cast overboard."

2. God gave very specific directions about which way the ship was to go. God's direction in our finances is always away from debt and toward prosperity. Debt is bondage. It is en-

slavement. It keeps us from being totally free to respond immediately when we are given an opportunity or when we confront a crisis.

Prosperity is having enough to handle any challenge or need that comes our way. God desires to meet our needs at this level, with a sufficient overflow to help others handle their needs and challenges.

3. God gave very specific promises about what would happen to people and goods. In this story, 276 men were spared. A ship was lost. God always places the value of people over things. There may be times in your life when you lose something that you perceive to be of value to you—perhaps a job, a home, a business, a vehicle, an heirloom. Always keep at the forefront of your thinking that God has promised to provide for your needs. Never mourn the loss of something to the detriment of a relationship. Never hold on to something if it means losing a person whom God has placed into your life, especially a child, a parent, a sibling, or a spouse.

In nearly all cases, as we seek God for His guidance about the material and financial provision we need in our lives—and especially our work and our material possessions—the Lord will show us ways in which we are to give so that He might take a portion of what we give and multiply an even greater blessing back to us. Expect God to be faithful to His laws regarding giving and receiving. Look for God's miracle provision.

PRAYING FOR GOD TO MEET YOUR NEEDS

The Bible has dozens of references to work as well as to giving and receiving. Let me share only a few of them with you to get you started:

- Give, and it shall be given unto you; good measure, pressed down, and shaken together, and running over, shall men give into your bosom. For with the same measure that ye mete withal it shall be measured to you again. (Luke 6:38)
- Give to him that asketh thee, and from him that would borrow of thee turn not thou away. (Matthew 5:42)
- The workman is worthy of his meat. (Matthew 10:10)
- One thing thou lackest: go thy way, sell whatsoever thou hast, and give to the poor, and thou shalt have treasure in heaven: and come, take up the cross, and follow me. (Mark 10:21)
- Behold, a sower went forth to sow; and when he sowed, some seeds . . . fell into good ground, and brought forth fruit, some an hundredfold, some sixtyfold, some thirtyfold. (Matthew 13:3–4, 8)

Praise and Thanksgiving for God's Provision

As you fast and pray, be sure to offer abundant thanks to God for the ways in which He has met financial and material needs in your life. Recall specific incidents.

Thank the Lord for:

- Putting generous people in your life.
- Giving you a job. Thank God for your employer and your position even if your employer and position are not ideal.
- Providing food, shelter, clothing, and warmth for you.

Praise God for the truth of James 1:17: "Every good gift and every perfect gift is from above, and cometh down from the Father of lights, with whom is no variableness, neither shadow of turning."

Praise God for His being the Multiplier of all good seed that you sow.

Praise God for His being the Source of all that you need.

Praise God for His being the Provider for you and your family.

Praise God for His giving you talents, energy, skills, and opportunities to work.

Praise God for the good work, good investment and business opportunities, and good income that you believe He has for you in your future.

Praying Specifically for Provision

In your petitions before the Lord regarding material and financial provision, ask the Lord first and foremost for two things:

1. A heart that is free of greed and selfishness. Ask the Lord to make you keenly aware that you must "love not the world, neither the things that are in the world." (1 John 2:15)
2. A heart that is generous toward those in need and toward the work of the Lord in preaching and teaching the gospel. Ask the Lord to remind you frequently that "he that doeth the will of God abideth for ever." (1 John 2:17)

Pray specifically for God to meet any financial need you have.

Pray specifically for the ability to reorder your priorities so that you can allocate your resources according to God's commandments. Pray that as you tithe and give offerings regularly, you will know how to use your remaining income to make wise purchases and investments.

14

RESTORING FAMILY RELATIONSHIPS

There's a little phrase in Isaiah 58 that people often overlook: "Hide not thyself from thine own flesh" (v. 7).

People today hide themselves in many ways from their own parents, children, or other blood relations. People hide themselves in even more ways from those who should be their spiritual brothers and sisters—those who are spiritually linked to them in every culture around the world because of the shed blood of Jesus Christ.

Some people hide themselves in their jobs, hobbies, or various clubs and activities, rarely spending time with their children. Some people hide themselves emotionally—they never disclose their true feelings, offer words of encouragement, or show signs of affection, all of which children, as well as adults, in a family desperately need. Still others hide themselves behind a wall of anger and bitterness, a wall of drunkenness, or a wall of addiction.

Within the body of Christ some hide from church by spending every weekend at their lake home . . . working late instead of going to midweek Bible study . . . or showing up at church events only on holidays or when a special musical program is being presented.

We need to recognize that the family is God's idea. He created it from the beginning, making Adam and Eve for each other and giving them children. The tribes of Israel were family tribes. The stories of the Bible describe virtually every type of family relationship—some pointing out to us the blessing of a healthy relationship, others the terrible consequences that can arise when a family relationship is unhealthy. Don't turn your back on your family! The Bible tells us plainly, "God setteth the solitary in families" (Ps. 68:6). Even those who are single are to be part of a "family" of close friends and loved ones.

THE FAST OF ESTHER AND MORDECAI

The book of Esther tells the story of a beautiful young orphan girl who rose from obscurity to become the queen of Persia. The day came, however, when a wicked counselor of the king, a man named Haman, decided that the time had come to act on his personal hatred of the Jews. He convinced the king to give him jurisdiction over the Jews and without fully realizing what he had done, the king gave Haman the power to "do with them as it seemeth good to thee" (Est. 3:11). Haman sent out a decree saying that on a particular day all Jews were to be destroyed.

Esther was a Jew. So was Mordecai. And when Mordecai read Haman's decree, he went to the king's gate clothed in sackcloth and ashes. There he sat, crying "with a loud and bitter cry" (Est. 4:1). Word came to Esther, who was in seclusion inside the palace, and she immediately sent word to find out why Mordecai was in such intense mourning. The messenger she sent came with this answer:

> Think not with thyself that thou shalt escape in the king's house, more than all the Jews. For if thou altogether holdest thy peace at this time, then shall there en-

largement and deliverance arise to the Jews from another place; but thou and thy father's house shall be destroyed: and who knoweth whether thou art come to the kingdom for such a time as this? (Esther 4:13–14)

The fact was, nobody in the king's court knew that Esther was a Jew. She might have been able to hide herself from her family, the Jewish people, at least temporarily. Esther, however, heeded the warning of Mordecai and sent word: "Go, gather together all the Jews that are present in Shushan, and fast ye for me, and neither eat nor drink three days, night or day: I also and my maidens will fast likewise; and so will I go in unto the king, which is not according to the law: and if I perish, I perish" (Est. 4:16).

Why did Esther think she might perish? Because at that time, she was somewhat estranged from her husband the king. The king had not called for her in some time and there was no real protocol for Esther to initiate a meeting with her husband.

What God did during this time of fasting and prayer was to reveal to Esther a multistage plan for going to the king on behalf of her family. First, she put on her royal robes and stood in the inner court of the king's house so that when the king sat on his throne he could see her standing there. She no doubt prayed as she stood in the court, hoping that the king would look upon her with favor and extend his scepter to her. That's exactly what happened. And when Esther drew near to the king and he asked, "What is thy request?" she presented the second stage of the plan God gave (Est. 5:3). She invited her husband and Haman to a banquet that night in her palace chambers.

During the banquet, the king asked Esther if she had any petitions. She had only one request, which was an invitation to come again to dinner the second night. At the second banquet, when Haman's guard was fully down and the king was fully enthralled once again with Esther's beauty and charm, the king asked Esther if she had any petitions. This time Esther spoke boldly: "Let my life be given me at my petition, and my people at my request: for we are sold, I and my people, to be destroyed, to be slain, and to perish. But if we had been sold for bondmen and bondwomen, I had held my tongue, although the enemy could not countervail the king's damage" (Est. 7:3–4).

The king asked who would dare do this to his queen, and Esther had the courage to name Haman. In the end, Haman and his family were destroyed, and Esther and Mordecai were promoted to great positions of government power in which they could enact decrees that not only furthered the goals of the Persian king but also brought great blessing to the Jews.

Esther did not hide herself from her family or her heritage. She became the rescuer of her people as a result.

PREPARING FOR THIS FAST

When we enter a time of fasting and praying that is related to our family ties, we need to be aware of some of the things that God desires for our families.

First, God desires that our families be saved. The Bible has a number of references to the salvation of entire households. After Lydia heard the message of Paul, she received Jesus as her Savior and "she was baptized, and her household" (Acts 16:15). After a powerful earthquake in Philippi, the bonds were broken that had held Paul and Silas captive in a prison cell. The two men, however, did not leave. The keeper of the prison came rushing in to see if his prisoners were still there and Paul and Silas had a wonderful opportunity to preach to him the word of the Lord. The keeper of the prison received Jesus as his Savior, washed the wounds of Paul and Silas, and then he "was baptized, he and all his, straightway." The rest of the night he spent rejoicing, "believing in God with all his house" (Acts 16:33–34).

One of the most important reasons for a season of fasting and praying is to seek God for the salvation of all your loved ones. Certainly we are to be bold in praying for our families' physical protection, especially in times of danger or persecution. More important, God calls us to be bold in praying that He will send preachers and witnesses to our loved ones so that they might hear the gospel, turn from their sins, receive the forgiveness made possible through the shed blood of Jesus, and commit their lives to following the Lord for the rest of their days.

Second, God desires that peace be established in your house. The Bible has numerous commands to refrain from anger, to treat one another with kindness, and to prefer one another rather than selfishly seeking one's own way. Some of the important reasons to fast and pray for your family include:

- Seeing lines of communication opened or improved.
- Seeing marriages restored.
- Seeing runaways come home.
- Seeing times of sorrow in a family turned into times of joy.
- Seeing greater understanding and empathy flow among family members.
- Seeing families come together with a renewed commitment to serve the Lord as a family.

Certainly Esther's courage bore seeds of peace. Through Esther and Mordecai, Haman's decree was reversed. Rather than an appointed death day, Esther set in motion a feast day called Purim, which continues to this day as a time of great celebration and the giving of gifts. It is a feast in which the Jews offer their praise to God for delivering them. Purim is set aside as a holy day to recall "the matters of the fastings and their cry" (Est. 9:31).

Peace . . . restoration . . . reconciliation . . . unity in faith . . . common goals . . . good communication . . . abiding love: these are the hallmarks of family that God desires for you and your loved ones.

Third, God desires for your family to experience the fullness of His blessings and to have influence for good on this earth. Because Esther did what she did on behalf of her family, her kinsman Mordecai was "next unto the king Ahasuerus, and great among the Jews, and accepted of the multitude of his brethren, seeking the wealth of his people, and speaking peace to all his seed" (Est. 10:3). Mordecai was put in a position that brought great blessing to his family, which included the blessing of wealth as well as peace.

Anticipating the Devil's Lies

As you begin to fast and pray for your family, you can expect the devil to come with some of his strongest lies. The devil has no desire to see Christian families flourish, or for Christian couples to bear children who might advance the kingdom of God on the earth. The enemy is likely to say to you:

- "Your family is so messed up that it can never be restored or healed."
- "Your family has been scattered and fragmented for so long, nothing will bring you together again."
- "Your marriage is marked by irreconcilable differences."
- "You and your children have never had a good relationship—what makes you think you can start having a good relationship with them now?"
- "You can never forgive your parents for what they did to you as a child. And why should you? What they did was unforgivable!"

Lies, lies, and more lies! Speak to the devil the truth of how much God desires for your family to be saved and to live in peace and purpose.

PRAYING FOR FAMILY WHOLENESS

Forgiveness is at the heart of both family salvation and family healing and reconciliation. A message of forgiveness is the foremost message that God desires for your family to represent to the world.

Each of us is wise to ask the Lord first and foremost to forgive us our sins—known and unknown, things we have done and things we have neglected to do. Ask for God's forgiveness for attitudes you have held, things you have said, things you have done, and even things you wish you would have done! Ask God to cleanse your heart of all desire for vengeance or retaliation.

Then ask the Lord to help you forgive and set free from your own heart any person who has hurt you, molested you, abused you, treated you unfairly, rejected you, maligned you, gossiped about you, or spoken harshly or unkindly to you. Ask the Lord to help you forgive any person who has trampled on your heart, either knowingly or unknowingly. Ask the Lord to help you forgive whether the person asks for forgiveness or not. (You may need to forgive someone who has already died. If so, ask the Lord to help you release that person from your heart and mind so old, hurtful memories can no longer tie you up in knots.)

Finally, ask the Lord to help you extend forgiveness to any person who may come to you and ask for it. Ask the Lord to help you be gracious and generous.

The Bible has numerous references to forgiveness, salvation, restoration, and reconciliation. I encourage you to consult a concordance and make a list of verses on these topics, and then look up one or more verses each day of your fast. Here are just a few verses that relate to forgiveness:

- Forgive, and ye shall be forgiven. (Luke 6:37)
- If ye forgive men their trespasses, your heavenly Father will also forgive you: but if ye forgive not men their trespasses,

neither will your Father forgive your trespasses. (Matthew 6:14–15)

- If we confess our sins, he is faithful and just to forgive us our sins, and to cleanse us from all unrighteousness. (1 John 1:9)
- For God so loved the world, that he gave his only begotten Son, that whosoever believeth in him should not perish, but have everlasting life. For God sent not his Son into the world to condemn the world; but that the world through him might be saved. (John 3:16–17)
- If my people, which are called by my name, shall humble themselves, and pray, and seek my face, and turn from their wicked ways; then will I hear from heaven, and will forgive their sin, and will heal their land. (2 Chronicles 7:14)

Praise and Thanksgiving for Your Family

As you praise and thank God for your family, voice the name of each family member to God individually. Praise God for the privilege of having each person in relationship with you. Thank God for the many gifts and talents He has put into each person . . . the ways in which He has used, prepared, and called each person . . . the ways in which He is using each person for His purposes on this earth . . . and the ways in which you know He desires to save, restore, heal, and bless all of your family members as they walk in the ways of the Lord and obey His commandments.

There really is no end to the thanksgiving and praise you can offer for your family! If you are anticipating marriage or having children one day, begin to thank and praise God for that future blessing. If your children are young, begin now to thank and praise God for preparing their futures and their future spouses and families.

Praise God for being the one who heals and restores all relationships from the inside out. Praise God for His saving power. Praise God for His desire to see you and your loved ones restored to godly fellowship. Praise God for the plans and purposes He has for you individually, and also as a family.

Not long ago a woman shared with me what she started doing for each of her children and grandchildren. She has a shelf of little blank books—one book for each child or grandchild. She had embossed in gold the name of the child or grandchild on the cover of the book. Inside the book, she was writing prayers as well as praises and thanksgivings. Some of her words of thanksgiving were linked to special experiences she shared with the child or grandchild. Some of her entries covered things that she was still believing would happen in the future of that child or grandchild.

What a special gift one day to each of these beloved people . . . and what a special tribute and memorial these books will be to a godly mother and grandmother. Even if you don't write down your prayers, praises, and thanksgiving for your family members, you can rest assured that your prayers, praises, and thanksgiving are recorded in heaven.

Praying Specifically for Your Family

One of the great prayers in the New Testament is a prayer that every person can pray freely and fully for each family member:

> For this cause we also, since the day we heard it, do not cease to pray for you, and to desire that ye might be filled with the knowledge of his will in all wisdom and spiritual understanding; that ye might walk worthy of the Lord unto all pleasing, being fruitful in every good work, and increasing in the knowledge of God; strengthened with all might, according to his glorious power, unto all patience and longsuffering with joyfulness; giving thanks unto the Father, which hath made us meet to be partakers of the inheritance of the saints in light: who hath delivered us from the power of dark-

ness, and hath translated us into the kingdom of his dear Son. (Colossians 1:9–13)

This prayer covers it all!

It covers a desire to see your loved ones walk in wisdom and understanding, truly trusting in and relying on God's guidance in all things.

It covers your loved ones' living lives marked by fruitfulness and spiritual maturity.

It covers your loved ones' developing spiritual power, persevering patience, and hearts filled with joy.

It covers personal salvation and deliverance from evil.

There are many specific things you might pray for each member of your family, but in praying for the details of things that may be temporary and bound to this earth, don't forget to pray for those things that are eternal and heavenly.

15

BRINGING HEALING SPEEDILY

Are you aware that the vast majority of diseases and ailments in the world today are related to what people take into their bodies? Viruses and bacteria produce only a small fraction of the deaths we have in the United States. Most heart disease, strokes, diabetes, and cancer deaths are related to people taking into their bodies the wrong substances, from hydrogenated fats to sugar, from nicotine to alcohol, from refined carbohydrates to drugs (both illegal substances and overuse of prescription medications). There are foods that are rooted firmly in what is good for us, and other foods that are evil to us. We have a choice to make about them.

In many ways, a fast wipes clean the food slate in our lives. Certainly fasting cleanses the digestive tract. It can also cleanse our thinking about food. When we fast, we are in a position of withdrawing from food so that once we go back to eating again, we can make clearer and better choices.

A woman who has been on various types of fasts recently said to me, "One of the main benefits to me of fasting is that it gets me off a treadmill of mindless eating. I have a tendency to eat without really thinking about what I'm eating. With my busy schedule it's too easy to pick up fast food products, which are usually junk food products. It's too easy to eat foods that are loaded with sugar and fat. When I fast, my addiction and craving for these foods is broken. And when I come out of a fast, I nearly always find that I have a strong desire for clean, whole foods. I thoroughly enjoy eating lightly steamed vegetables—actually, I find that I am able to taste vegetables again, rather than the butter and salt I was covering them with. I enjoy eating a piece of fresh fruit. These foods are satisfying to me. Overall, I am far more conscious about what I am eating and I am far more disciplined in making food choices that are good for me."

What a wonderful physical benefit this can be to a person. Beyond these physical benefits related directly to food choices are the emotional and spiritual issues related to food intake.

Anorexia, bulimia, obesity, food allergies, and food addictions are all various forms of evil that are associated with food. Underlying these issues we often find emotional issues related to the reasons that people overeat, undereat, or continue to eat things that they know—in their minds, but not necessarily in their hearts—are wrong for them. Fasting causes a person to address the underlying evils associated with poor eating.

And yet there's still more that's related to food. We need food to live. When we abstain from food, we are chastening our spirits before God. We are humbling ourselves before the Lord and crucifying the appetites of the flesh and denying them rule over our lives. The psalmist spoke of humbling and chastening his soul with fasting (Ps. 35:13, 69:10). Fasting demonstrates a mastery over the appetites of man. In this regard, there's a healing that relates to our soul and spirit.

Healing and Fasting

Healing and fasting have been linked for literally thousands of years, not only in the Bible but in general world history. Hippocrates was an outstanding physician in his time. He is called the "father of modern medicine" and the Hippocratic Oath that he set as a standard physicians today still follow.

I find it interesting that the Hippocratic statement titled "On the Physician" gives detailed instructions about how to prepare an operating room, the arrangement of natural and artificial light, the need to have clean hands and instruments, the proper position of patients for various procedures, and the bandaging of wounds. Hippocrates taught people to rely upon diet and exercise more than upon drugs. He often prescribed fasting. He also taught that man should eat only one meal a day.

Many assume that a person should not fast if he is sick. In some cases, that is true. In other cases, a fast can be very helpful in furthering the healing process or in cleansing the body of harmful substances that promote obesity-related diseases. For example, one of the best things a person can do in times of fever or serious diarrhea is to modify their diet to lighter foods like fruits, soups, and liquids in general. It's important that a person stay hydrated—drinking sufficient water (fortified with electrolytes) and consuming foods with high water content. Even so, giving the body's digestive system a rest as it battles viral or bacterial infection can be very helpful. (Before commencing a fast, you should assess your health and consider visiting a health professional.)

As I have studied nutrition, I found it very interesting that refined white sugar was first labeled with a skull and crossbones because it was thought to be a poison to the body. Other foods, such as fatty red meat, have been linked to disease. In recent decades, the food laws in the Old Testament have been subjected to a number of scientific studies and in virtually all cases, the foods in question have been shown to have potential for physical harm owing to the toxins and bacteria often harbored in the forbidden foods.

We need to become knowledgeable about foods and various practices that make us sick. We need to fast from those foods or substances at all times, not just some of the time.

THE HEALTH BENEFITS OF FASTING

There are at least five major health benefits to fasting.

1. Fasting Gives the Body's Organs a Rest

Are you aware that most of the calories that you take in every day you spend not in exercise, but in digesting food and dispersing nutrients throughout the body? When a person fasts, he allows the organs of his body to rest and in a time of rest, to rejuvenate and renew at the cellular level.

2. Fasting Aids the Healing Process

God designed our bodies to heal first at the cellular level. The way in which our cells work is one of life's most intricate mysteries. It is in the cells that we are nourished. It is also at the cellular level that waste products and toxins are eliminated. It is believed by many that fasting helps to unclog a variety of systems in the body, but mostly, it helps clear away poisons in our cells.

Many believe that a three-week fast can help lower cholesterol levels in the blood, lower blood pressure, give relief from arthritis, and help greatly with weight loss. People who fast seem to have an elevated production of cells that kill tumor cells. Some have found relief from rheumatoid arthritis and joint pain and stiffness. One common area of healing is an improvement in allergies, especially those linked to foods.

3. Fasting Has a Calming Effect on the Emotions and Mind

Studies have shown that a wide variety of symptoms improve dramatically in those who suffer from such things as hyperactivity, dyslexia, schizophrenia, depression, and even autism. Part of the improvement in these conditions may come from the fact that in a fast, both the body and brain tissues are cleansed of toxins.

4. Fasting Breaks Food Addictions

Many people don't realize that they are addicted to certain foods or substances. But if you take away their caffeine, sugar, or fat, they go through withdrawal symptoms that are not unlike the symptoms of drug withdrawal.

A woman said to me, "I once drank a great deal of coffee. I wasn't aware that I was drinking as much coffee as I was until my secretary one day asked in the middle of the afternoon if I wanted her to make a third pot of coffee. When I registered surprise that we had gone through two whole pots of coffee that day, she replied, 'You're the only one drinking it.' I was shocked. So I decided to quit drinking caffeinated coffee overnight.

"I've never had such a fierce headache or nausea. I also realized that I had been on a perpetual high—and without caffeine, I hit a real low. I felt like the people I had once seen in a movie about heroin addiction! I quickly shifted gears and over a three-month period, I weaned myself off of so much caffeine. Now, years later, I drink only one to two cups of coffee a day, and those cups are made with a fifty-fifty mix of caffeinated and decaffeinated coffee."

As you address food addictions in your life, you may have moments when you feel weak. As I've mentioned, you may have a slight headache or be irritable for a day or two. You may also have bad breath, experience frequent urination, or feel a sensation of coolness. You may have bouts of sleeplessness. When these symptoms occur, recognize that you are breaking an addiction. You are in recovery. You are not getting sick as you might think—rather, you are in the process of getting well!

5. Fasting Breaks an Emotional Dependency on Food

In this case, a person's emotional health is being healed even as the body is being cleansed.

Fasting forces a person to come to grips with what is real hunger and what is a perceived need to eat. So many of us eat strictly out of habit. The clock strikes noon and we think, *Time to eat!* It doesn't matter if we are truly hungry or not.

In the first few days of a fast, a person may feel hunger pangs from time to time. This is usually the body's way of announcing that the stomach is empty. If a person is drinking sufficient water, he greatly lessens these pangs. After a few days, however, as the body begins to use the fat that is stored in the cells and tissues of the body, feelings of hunger usually diminish greatly. The real battle is in the mind. The mind often continues to think about food. This creates an emotion-based, idea-based hunger that is not real physical hunger.

Researchers have studied the difference between emotion-based or idea-based hunger and real hunger. They have found that people can fast for fairly long periods of time without experiencing real hunger. This is especially true for people who have large reserves of stored fat. Once real hunger begins to surface, however, it is time for a person to quit fasting and to begin reintroducing food to the body.

The benefit to the person who is fasting is this: he comes face-to-face with the truth that the primary reason he eats is mental and emotional, not physical. We eat to be social, to feel satisfied emotionally, and to feel in control. We rarely eat because we truly are physically hungry. In fact, we tend to eat long after we are physically satisfied. Our brains just haven't been given the opportunity to catch up with what our bodies are trying to tell us.

One of the best things a person can do after a fast is to eat a few bites and then wait fifteen minutes to see if he is still physically hungry. In most cases, the few bites will have been sufficient.

Having a mastery over food intake ultimately results in a person's feeling emotionally stronger and even more in control of life. In this way, a person experiences an emotional healing— he has a renewed inner strength that comes from knowing: I don't have to eat to have value. *I don't have to be full to be fulfilled!*

PREPARING FOR THIS FAST

As you prepare to go into a fast for the purpose of physical cleansing or healing, refer to the practical information presented earlier in this book. Prepare your body in advance for the fast. Here are some additional steps:

First, consult a physician if you have any questions or qualms about the fast you desire to undertake. Work with a physician who understands the benefits of fasting, and preferably the spiritual discipline of fasting and praying.

Second, be very aware of any negative health symptoms that might linger after the first few days of a long fast. If you experience any heart palpitations or chest pain, any severe muscle cramping that doesn't go away after drinking a glass of water, a severe headache that lingers, or any other serious health problem, consult a physician about how to proceed safely or how to break your fast safely.

Third, alert your family to the fact that you are going to be fasting and praying. Ask them not to talk to you about food or about special meals they might be having outside your home. Ask them not to nag you or criticize you about the fact that you are fasting. Ask for their help and assistance, and especially ask them to recognize that your primary purpose in fasting is to seek God for His divine health plan. Ask them to take over meal preparation chores—or better yet, to join you in the fast.

Fourth, go into a season of fasting and praying for healing with very clear goals about the health that you believe God desires for you to experience. Ask the Lord in your prayer times what other things you might do in your life to enhance the healing process of your body, soul, and spirit.

Anticipating the Devil's Lies

The enemy will come to you with a variety of arguments about why fasting is a bad idea for your health. Don't be surprised when he whispers into your mind:

- "This is the worst thing you could do for your health."
- "Fasting is harmful more than helpful."
- "Only well people should fast, and you are certainly not strong enough or well enough to fast."
- "Food is good for you, not bad for you. God wants you to have what's good."

Lies, lies, and more lies! Separate truth from lie and confront the devil with the truth.

PRAYING FOR TOTAL HEALING

I strongly encourage you to consult a concordance and make a personal list of Bible verses and passages that focus on God's healing power. A well-known evangelist once told me that when he meets with people in quiet, one-on-one settings to pray for them he always begins by reading a passage of the Bible that tells of a healing miracle. This evangelist said, "I read especially about the healing miracles of Jesus and then I say to the person, 'What Jesus did for that person, He wants to do for you.'"

That's the real key, isn't it? It isn't enough to read about healing. We must say to ourselves as we read about God's healing power: *This is for me! God doesn't change. He doesn't play favorites. What He has done for others, He can and will do for me!* We must see the Bible's promises of healing as being for us and for our loved ones.

Here are just a few verses to encourage you:

- And Jesus went about all Galilee, teaching in their synagogues, and preaching the gospel of the kingdom, and healing all manner of sickness and all manner of disease among the people. (Matthew 4:23)
- Bless the LORD, O my soul, and forget not all his benefits . . . who healeth all thy diseases. (Psalm 103:2–3)
- Heal me, O LORD, and I shall be healed; save me, and I shall be saved: for thou art my praise. (Jeremiah 17:14)
- Have mercy upon me, O LORD; for I am weak; O LORD, heal me: for my bones are vexed. . . . The LORD hath heard my supplication; the LORD will receive my prayer. (Psalm 6:2, 9)

Praise and Thanksgiving as You Seek Healing

Most of us have been sick or injured countless times in our lives—perhaps at the level of having a cold or a scraped knee, or perhaps with a serious injury or disease. It's amazing, isn't it, how many times God has already healed us? Give Him thanks for the healing work He has done in your life through the years. Be very specific in offering your thanksgiving. In doing so, you will be reminding your own brain and body that God's healing processes have worked, are working, and will continue to work in you!

- "Thank You, Heavenly Father, for Your desire to heal me and make me whole."
- "Thank You, Heavenly Father, for the ways in which You are already directing me and will continue to direct me toward the information, medical assistance, and spiritual assistance that can help me to live in the best health possible."
- "Thank You, Heavenly Father, for the ways in which You are giving my body and my brain rest, and for the ways in which You are healing my emotions, during this time of fasting."

Praise the Lord for being your Healer! Ultimately all healing comes from God. Many highly skilled and highly qualified physicians openly acknowledge that truth. Medicines and various medical procedures may put us into a better position to be healed, but God is the Author of all healing. He is the Source of life—He is the one who causes our hearts to beat, our lungs to inflate, our strength to be renewed, our energy to be restored, our tissues to knit together, our cells to be rejuvenated and replaced. Praise God for the ways in which He has created you and continues to re-create you physically.

Those who are seeking the protection of the Lord often recite Psalm 91. I believe this is also a wonderful psalm to recite repeatedly in times of sickness, as you are confronting a disease, or as you are recovering from an injury or surgery. Read this psalm aloud to the Lord as a praise offering.

Praying Specifically for Healing

Ask the Lord very boldly and specifically for your healing and to help you to establish a healthful way of living.

Ask the Lord to guide you into making the right choices about foods and to give you the information you need about which foods contribute most to good health.

Ask the Lord to free you from any addictions you have to food and to free you from any emotional attachments you have to food.

Ask the Lord to fulfill the words of Psalm 91:15–16 in your life: "He shall call upon me, and I will answer him: I will be with him in trouble; I will deliver him, and honour him. With long life will I satisfy him, and shew him my salvation."

PRAYING AND FASTING
FOR REVIVAL

The three final purposes for fasting in Isaiah 58 are related to spiritual revival. Even though Isaiah 58 is an Old Testament passage, the truths in this chapter definitely relate to our extending the gospel of Jesus Christ and the kingdom of God on earth:

- Light breaking forth as the morning.
- Establishing a path of righteousness.
- Revealing the glory of the Lord.

Each of these reasons to pray and fast is rooted in a recognition and confession of sin, repentance, and spiritual renewal. This happens on an individual basis. It also happens in families and churches that pray and fast as a body of believers.

At the very core of all reasons to pray and fast is a desire to be in closer relationship with the Lord. We must never lose sight of the fact that God does not honor the rebellious. He will have absolutely nothing to do with sin—He never causes a person to sin or leads a person into temptation to sin. God loves sinners, but He removes Himself completely from sinful situations, sinful relationships, and sinful environments.

Rather, the Lord continually calls us to ongoing renewal and to greater depths of relationship with Him. That's what revival is all about. The revived heart has renewed energy, renewed commitment to win souls to Christ Jesus, renewed vision for what God desires to do on the earth, renewed commitment to being part of God's answer to a hurting world, and renewed awareness of God at work in all things at all times and always for His glory.

THE PROCLAMATION OF JESUS AS THE SAVIOR

Revival is always rooted in the proclamation of the gospel of Jesus Christ. And what are the elements of that gospel that revive the spirit of man? Here are some of them:

- We can be forgiven of our sins—and freed from all past sins and the guilt and shame associated with them. (1 John 1:9)
- We can receive eternal life. (John 3:16)
- We can receive a new nature that desires to turn away from sin and obey the commands of God.
- We can receive the gift of God's Holy Spirit, who enables us to walk in truth and clearly discern right from wrong—the Spirit empowers us to have godly character and live godly lives as vessels through which the Spirit pours His gifts and power.
- We can take authority over evil.
- We can see our prayers answered more readily and positively because we have an ability to pray in the Spirit according to the will of the Father. (John 15:7)

The person who receives Jesus Christ as Savior is a person who is in position to have a wonderful relationship with God! The Bible tells us:

His divine power has given us everything we need for life and godliness through our knowledge [by interaction] of him [relationship] who called us by his own glory and goodness. Through these he has given us his very great and precious promises [principles], that through them you may participate in the divine nature [power] and escape corruption in the world caused by evil desires. (2 Peter 1:3–4 NIV)

As you read through the Bible, you will see this pattern surface time and time again. A relationship with God and a life in obedience to God's principles produces manifestations of the power of God.

Prayer and fasting call us to deepen our relationship with God. They call us to examine our lives and to see where we are failing to obey God's principles. In times of prayer and fasting a person is nearly always convicted by the Holy Spirit of areas in which he needs to better obey. As a person knows the heart of God better and comes into greater alignment with God's commands, the power of God naturally begins to flow in that person's life. With the flow of God's presence and power, a person truly is revived.

16

THE BREAKING FORTH
OF LIGHT

We've all heard the phrase, "I've seen the light!" Seeing with renewed vision is a very good purpose for fasting. The person who
prays and fasts often has a new clarity about not only the current reality of a situation, but what God desires to be the reality!

Prayer and fasting also make a person much more keenly
aware of what is missing or sinful in any situation or relationship. A person who prays and fasts regularly develops an increasingly accurate ability to discern what he needs to make
pure for God's eyes. What may not have felt like a sin to a person at the time he was born again he may very well clearly identify as sin the closer he draws to the Lord. In this sense, a person
who prays and fasts not only "sees the light" but "shines the
light" so that the full truth of murky, shadowy, and ungodly behaviors and compromises are revealed for what they truly are.

DANIEL'S FAST AND REVELATION

One of the most stunning chapters about fasting and praying in
the entire Bible is Daniel 9. Daniel was in Babylon, where he had
been taken captive as a young man. He rose to great power and

authority under the Babylonian kings because God gave him a tremendous ability to interpret dreams and make wise judgments. Then the time came when God gave Daniel a very powerful, vivid vision that he did not understand. The vision was so real and so awesome that Daniel "fainted, and was sick" for a period of time (Dan. 8:27). He was utterly astonished at the vision and did not understand any of it. He knew only that it had to do with the future. He also knew what the prophet Jeremiah had prophesied about the number of years the children of Israel would be in captivity.

Daniel desired that the light of understanding be shed on what he had seen. He set his face unto the Lord God, "to seek by prayer and supplications, with fasting, and sackcloth, and ashes" (Dan. 9:3).

This passage from Daniel may seem long—sixteen verses— but I want you to read it carefully. I recommend that you read it aloud. In fact, read through it several times and underline key words and phrases that may seem especially relevant to you. This is the prayer Daniel prayed during his fast, which eventually lasted three weeks. It is a prayer that should be the focal point for our churches today as we pray for revival. It is also a prayer that any person can pray for revival in his own life or in his family.

> I prayed unto the LORD my God, and made my confession, and said, O Lord, the great and dreadful God, keeping the covenant and mercy to them that love him, and to them that keep his commandments; we have sinned, and have committed iniquity, and have done wickedly, and have rebelled, even by departing from thy precepts and from thy judgments: neither have we hearkened unto thy servants the prophets, which spake in thy name to our kings, our princes, and our fathers, and to all the people of the land.

O Lord, righteousness belongeth unto thee, but unto us confusion of faces, as at this day; to the men of Judah, and to the inhabitants of Jerusalem, and unto all Israel, that are near, and that are far off, through all the countries whither thou hast driven them, because of their trespass that they have trespassed against thee.

O Lord, to us belongeth confusion of face, to our kings, to our princes, and to our fathers, because we have sinned against thee.

To the Lord our God belong mercies and forgiveness, though we have rebelled against him; neither have we obeyed the voice of the LORD our God, to walk in his laws, which he set before us by his servants the prophets.

Yea, all Israel have transgressed thy law, even by departing, that they might not obey thy voice; therefore the curse is poured upon us, and the oath that is written in the law of Moses the servant of God, because we have sinned against him.

And he hath confirmed his words which he spake against us, and against our judges that judged us, by bringing upon us a great evil: for under the whole heaven hath not been done as hath been done upon Jerusalem.

As it is written in the law of Moses, all this evil is come upon us: yet made we not our prayer before the LORD our God, that we might turn from our iniquities, and understand thy truth.

Therefore hath the LORD watched upon the evil, and brought it upon us: for the LORD our God is righteous in all his works which he doeth: for we obeyed not his voice.

And now, O Lord our God, that hast brought thy people forth out of the land of Egypt with a mighty hand, and has gotten thee renown, as at this day; we have sinned, we have done wickedly.

O Lord, according to all thy righteousness, I beseech thee, let thine anger and thy fury be turned away from thy city Jerusalem, thy holy mountain: because for our sins, and for the iniquities of our fathers, Jerusalem and thy people are become a reproach to all that are about us.

Now therefore, O our God, hear the prayer of thy servant, and his supplications, and cause thy face to shine upon thy sanctuary that is desolate, for the Lord's sake.

O my God, incline thine ear; and hear; open thine eyes, and behold our desolations, and the city which is called by thy name: for we do not present our supplications before thee for our righteousness, but for thy great mercies.

O Lord, hear; O Lord, forgive; O Lord, hearken and do; defer not, for thine own sake, O my God: for thy city and thy people are called by thy name. (Daniel 9:4–19)

There are several things I want to call your attention to in this prayer.

First, Daniel confessed his sins and the sins of his people. He did not run from the fact that it was on account of the Israelites' sins that they found themselves in Babylon. He didn't blame the Babylonians. He knew they were not God's chosen people and therefore they did not know right from wrong. It was the Babylonians' nature to sin. The sin of Israel was something else. The Israelites knew what was wrong before the Lord and they had done it anyway.

Daniel acknowledged that the issue of sin was not a behavior issue as much as it was a heart-nature issue. The people had rebelled . . . behaved wickedly . . . refused to obey the law . . . refused to hear the words of the prophets. As a result they were experiencing great confusion—in other words, they had been scattered across the face of the earth. Most of all, Daniel acknowledged that they had not heeded the voice of the Lord and they had not gone before the Lord to ask for God's mercy and forgiveness.

One of the reasons I asked you to read through this lengthy passage is this: so often people think that to confess their sins they simply need to come before the Lord and say, "I'm sorry. I messed up. Please forgive me. And now let me ask You for what I want. . . ." Daniel described *how* the people had sinned, and this is important for us to do if we are truly to understand how we got into the mess in which we find ourselves, individually as well as in our families and in our nation. We need to recognize before God that we have not kept God's commandments or followed His directives in our lives. We need to stop blaming other people, institutions, the times, cultural trends, or any other thing. We need to look in the mirror and say, "I have sinned."

Second, Daniel cast himself on the mercy of the Lord. He recognized that the Lord did not need to forgive him or his people. Too often we don't fully recognize our need of God's mercy. God is under no obligation to us—rather, we are under obligation to Him. Part of Daniel's prayer acknowledged that all power and authority were in God's hands.

Third, Daniel offered praise to the Lord. He declared the righteousness of the Lord, the Lord's mighty hand in delivering the Israelites from the Egyptians, and that the Lord alone was worthy of all that He had done for the children of Israel. We, too, must acknowledge the sovereignty and holiness of God.

Fourth and finally, Daniel asked the Lord to hear his prayer, to forgive the people, and to reverse their captivity. Most of Daniel's prayer was in confession and praise. His petitions were very few.

What happens when we pray this way? First, we have light shed on ourselves. We understand more clearly our position before the Lord and our need of a Savior. We understand more clearly why we are suffering in some of the ways we are suffering. We recognize the deceptiveness of our own hearts.

Second, we have light shed on the awesome nature of Almighty God.

Before we ever make a petition to God in a time of fasting and prayer, it is very important that we understand clearly who God is, who we are, and the accurate status of our relationship with God.

As we discover that we need to confess our sins and seek God's forgiveness—something we all need at all times—then we need to confess our sins.

As we see ways in which we have broken our relationship with God, we need to own up to our error and ask for God's forgiveness.

As we have our eyes opened to the vastness of God's love and mercy, and to the infinite nature of God's wisdom and power, we must cast ourselves fully on God's care of us.

As we open our eyes to see clearly our need, we must humbly ask for God's help.

Although a person who has never accepted Jesus as Savior may not recognize all of this as he or she responds to the anointed preaching of God's Word, all of these elements are present in salvation and revival.

The only position we can have before the Lord is a position of utter humility and dependency. Those are the very positions to which a fast leads. We recognize as we fast that we are totally dependent upon God for all things at all times.

What happened as the outcome to Daniel's prayer and fasting? Daniel wrote that even while he was praying to God, the angel Gabriel showed up. He informed Daniel and talked with him, saying, "O Daniel, I am now come forth to give thee skill and understanding. . . . I am come to shew thee; for thou art greatly beloved: therefore understand the matter, and consider the vision" (Dan. 9:22–23).

Daniel received the light he desired. He also received tremendous affirmation of God's love for him. These are two outcomes we, too, can expect as we go before the Lord in fasting and prayer.

PREPARING FOR THIS FAST

As you prepare to fast before the Lord for spiritual renewal and revival:

First, focus on what Jesus did for you on the cross. Put yourself once again in a place of total dependency upon the Lord.

Second, recognize that there may be things you don't know about yourself, and there certainly are things that you don't know about God. Open yourself to learning all you can in your time of prayer and fasting.

Third, anticipate God's word to you that will give you understanding. Anticipate that God's love will be shed abroad in your heart in a way that you will know without a shadow of doubt that you are His beloved child now and forever.

Anticipating the Devil's Lies

The devil, of course, has absolutely no interest in seeing any person saved, renewed or revived spiritually, growing spiritually, gaining understanding about the purposes of God, or feeling God's love! He will come to lie to you:

- "God doesn't *really* love you. You've disappointed and disobeyed Him too many times."
- "You've sinned too much and your sins have been too big for God to ever forgive you."
- "You didn't really sin. What you did was totally justified."
- "You don't deserve anything that has happened to you. It's all somebody else's fault."

Lies, lies, and more lies! God always stands ready to love, forgive, and renew a person who is truly humble and repentant.

PRAYING THAT GOD'S LIGHT WILL SHINE BRIGHTLY

Wonderful verses in both the Old and New Testaments speak of God's love and the light of God. Here are just a few of them to claim for your life:

- In him [Jesus] was life; and the life was the light of men. . . . As many as received him, to them gave he power to become the sons of God, even to them that believe on his name. (John 1:4, 12)
- This is the condemnation, that light is come into the world, and men loved darkness rather than light, because their deeds were evil. For every one that doeth evil hateth the light, neither cometh to the light, lest his deeds should be reproved. But he that doeth truth cometh to the light, that his deeds may be made manifest, that they are wrought in God. (John 3:19–21)
- Then spake Jesus again unto them, saying, "I am the light of the world: he that followeth me shall not walk in darkness, but shall have the light of life." (John 8:12)
- God, who commanded the light to shine out of darkness, hath shined in our hearts, to give the light of the knowledge of the glory of God in the face of Jesus Christ. (2 Cor. 4:6)

Praise and Thanksgiving for God's Light

As you pray and fast, thank the Lord frequently for the many insights into His Word that He has given you, is giving you, and will give you as you study your Bible.

- "Thank You, Heavenly Father, for what You are showing me."
- "Thank You, Heavenly Father, for what You are teaching me."
- "Thank You, Heavenly Father, for the ways You have and are convicting me so I might put away my sins and obey You more fully."
- "Thank You, Heavenly Father, for Your patience and mercy toward me."

Praise the Lord that He is the giver of:

- Life.
- Light.
- Revelation and insight.
- Salvation and revival.

There are countless ways and reasons for you to give thanks and praise to the Lord for the salvation of your eternal spirit. The book of Revelation tells us that the throne room of God is filled with pure and unending light: "There shall be no night there; and they need no candle, neither light of the sun; for the Lord God giveth them light" (Rev. 22:5). It is in this glorious light that we will join the angels and all other creatures in a great praise song. It's a song we can begin singing today: "Worthy is the Lamb that was slain to receive power, and riches, and wisdom, and strength, and honour, and glory, and blessing" (Rev. 5:12).

Praying Specifically for His Light

As you pray and fast, you should feel free to ask the Lord any question you desire to ask Him. Be committed, however, to waiting on His answer. His answer may not come right away. Remember that Daniel had to wait three weeks in fasting for an answer to come.

Ask the Lord questions about:

- Your life—and why you have been through some of the things you've been through.
- Your current problems—and why you are experiencing them.
- His plan for you—who He desires you become and what He wants you to accomplish on this earth.
- Your motivations—the reasons why you respond to some things the way you do.
- Who He desires to be in your life and what He desires to do for you.

Listen closely.
Listen quietly.
Listen until He answers you.

17

ESTABLISHING A PATH
OF RIGHTEOUSNESS

One of the things that God desires to do for every person who prays and fasts is to direct that person's footsteps in the path of righteousness. This is the path through life in which God reveals His will and we obey His commands. It is a path that leads to tremendous blessings, and ultimately, to eternal life.

Every one of us has difficulty at some point in life staying on the path. The Bible tells us that we all sin and that we are fooling ourselves if we say we don't. The first letter of John says: "If we say that we have no sin, we deceive ourselves, and the truth is not in us. . . . If we say that we have not sinned, we make him [Jesus] a liar, and his word is not in us" (1 John 1:8, 10).

Sometimes we stray off the path because we are chasing our own dreams, not God's. Sometimes we can't see the path clearly because our sin has dimmed our ability to discern God's ways. Sometimes we fall into a pit because we willfully choose to rebel against God.

The good news is that God in His mercy rescues us from our own disobedience when we truly seek to return to Him and live according to His commands. The psalmist knew this and wrote:

My prayer is unto thee, O LORD . . . in the multitude of
thy mercy hear me, in the truth of thy salvation. Deliver
me out of the mire, and let me not sink: let me be delivered from them that hate me, and out of the deep waters. . . . Hear me, O LORD; for thy lovingkindness is
good: turn unto me according to the multitude of thy
tender mercies. (Psalm 69:13–14, 16)

JOHN THE BAPTIST: A LIFE OF FASTING

A man whose name is nearly synonymous with a call to righteousness is John the Baptist. From his birth, John was devoted
wholly to serving the Lord and to calling people to repentance
and revival. The Bible tells us, "In those days came John the Baptist, preaching in the wilderness of Judaea, and saying, Repent
ye: for the kingdom of heaven is at hand. For this is he that was
spoken of by the prophet Esaias, saying, The voice of one crying
in the wilderness, Prepare ye the way of the Lord, make his paths
straight" (Matt. 3:1–5).

John did not only call people to righteousness, of course. He
lived a righteous life and by the example of his life, he attracted
many people as his followers—not only those who came to repent and be baptized by him, but people who came to learn
from him and become more like him.

John was a person who lived as a Nazirite, and he had done
so from birth. The word *Nazirite* comes from the word that
means "to vow." Those who lived by the Nazirite vows, as we've
seen, were people who kept very strict rules about what they ate
and wore, and how long they let their hair grow. We find these
rules in Numbers 6:2–8:

If any of you want to dedicate yourself to me by vow-
ing to become a Nazirite, you must no longer drink
any wine or beer or use any kind of vinegar. Don't

drink grape juice or eat grapes or raisins—not even the seeds or skins. Even the hair of a Nazirite is sacred to me, and as long as you are a Nazirite, you must never cut your hair. . . . You must never go close to a dead body, not even that of your father, mother, brother, or sister. That would make you unclean. Your hair is the sign that you are dedicated to me, so remain holy. (CEV)

John was known as a man who "had his raiment of camel's hair, and a leather girdle about his loins; and his meat was locusts and wild honey" (Matt. 3:4).

John's disciples were well known for fasting often, and for being people of prayer. They certainly must have learned this from John, who was obviously a man who did not drink or eat any grape products, but who did eat locusts and wild honey. "Locusts" may have been insects—which were common food at that time and are actually a rich source of protein. "Locusts" may also have referred to carob seeds, which appear in shape, size, and color to be like locusts—again, these seeds are a rich source of nutrients. Honey and honeycomb are also very healthful foods.

I found it interesting to learn a number of years ago about an island off South Korea in which a village of elderly people boast that some of their women live to be two hundred years old by eating locusts and honey. They grind up locusts, mix them with honey, and sell the mixture in jars to tourists. Their claims have never been verified scientifically, but many elderly people do live in that village and perhaps what they sell does represent what John the Baptist ate. We cannot know that with certainty, but what we can know is this: the fast that John the Baptist kept as part of his very disciplined life was a partial fast that eliminated most foods and was based on very few foods.

Eliminating Much and Clinging to Basics

Can you see the link between the eating style of John the Baptist and a lifestyle of righteousness? Both involve eliminating many things and clinging to a few vitally important things.

John eliminated most foods from his diet. If we truly are to live righteous lives, God is going to call us to eliminate a great deal from our lives. In Exodus 19:5, He calls us to be a distinct people. The King James Version uses the phrase "peculiar treasure," but here "peculiar" does not mean weird—it means a people set apart from the world. We are to be unique. Now, we may appear a little strange to the world because we don't think the way the world thinks, talk the way the world talks, or do many of the things that the world does. So be it! We are God's treasure.

While eliminating most foods from his diet, John did eat what was nourishing and gave health to his body. This, too, is a picture of the righteous path. We are to partake in those things that truly are of benefit to us, not just in the short run of our lives but for all eternity. We are to stick to the narrow way that Jesus described when He said: "Enter ye in at the strait gate: for wide is the gate, and broad is the way, that leadeth to destruction, and many there be which go in thereat: because strait is the gate, and narrow is the way, which leadeth unto life, and few there be that find it" (Matt. 7:13–14).

What Is It That Keeps Us from Righteousness?

The simple answer to that question is sin. But what is it that causes us to sin? The Bible tells us that we face three great temptations (see 1 John 2:16):

1. *The lust of the flesh.* These are the human drives and impulses that cause us to overindulge and to seek more and more gratification for the flesh. These human drives include primarily a sex drive that turns from what God intended for

marriage into unbridled lust, and a drive for food and drink that becomes gluttony. These normal human drives become the lust of the flesh when our appetites for sex, food, and drink grow out of control and can never be satisfied.

2. *The lust of the eyes.* This is a human drive to acquire things and occasionally to acquire people because we see them as things. The lust of the eyes results in greed and abuse.

3. *The pride of life.* This is a human drive for power over other people—a drive to be recognized above other people, to be acknowledged and applauded above other people, and to be worshiped by other people.

It isn't the devil alone who tempts us in these things. Most temptations arise from our own lusts and pride. And, in some cases, we crave the affection and attention of people so much that we easily give in to peer temptations. As a man once said, "I can resist all pressure except peer pressure."

Jesus said plainly that we cannot love two masters—the world and the Father. We must choose (see Matt. 6:24).

A Purifying Process

Several passages in the Bible refer to God's purifying process in our lives. Zechariah 13:9 tells us, "I . . . will refine them as silver is refined, and will try them as gold is tried: they shall call on my name, and I will hear them: I will say, It is my people: and they shall say, The LORD is my God." In just one verse, God gave us the basics for what it means to walk in righteousness. No person is made perfect, complete, or whole in a moment. God lays before us a process of refinement in which we walk increasingly in the righteousness of Jesus Christ. A strengthening, renewing, reviving, purifying process is a central part of our being established in righteousness.

A refiner's fire is hot, and sometimes the conviction of the Holy Spirit is searing in our lives. We feel His heat to make changes. That may be what leads us to a time of praying and fasting. If so, allow the Holy Spirit to do His work in you. Be open to all ways in which He may show you how He desires to purify your life and establish you so that you cannot be moved when it comes to your faithful witness of the Lord Jesus Christ.

Get Ready for a Fresh Anointing

Fasting for the purpose of establishing righteousness often results in a fresh anointing from the Holy Spirit. Jesus taught:

> No man puts a piece of new cloth unto an old garment, for that which is put in to fill it up taketh from the garment, and the rent is made worse. Neither do men put new wine into old bottles: else the bottles break and the wine runneth out, and the bottles perish: but they put new wine into new bottles, and both are preserved. (Matthew 9:16–17)

I once heard about a person who had stored a gallon of apple cider in a cupboard and forgot about it. It began to ferment. One day an explosion sent that cider spewing all over the inside of the cupboard! Just as a container cannot hold fermenting cider, so old wineskins cannot hold the expansion of fermenting wine—the skins crack and break under the pressure from the inside.

The Lord always has something new for us. This doesn't mean we turn away from the Bible or the teachings and traditions that have deep meaning in the church. It means that the Holy Spirit is continually working in us to do God's new thing.

Jesus gave this particular teaching in the context of fasting. What is He saying to us? I believe one of the main lessons is that fasting produces a new anointing in our lives. It brings about a fresh revelation of the Holy Spirit . . . a renewed enthusiasm for the things of God . . . an infusion of spiritual energy and power that we call *the anointing*.

One of the ways in which old wineskins were made like new again was by a vineyard keeper's rubbing oil into them. This made them softer and more pliable, able to expand and contain the new wine. *To anoint* means "to rub on." Shepherds anointed their sheep with oil to repel bugs and to protect wounds from infection.

As we fast and pray, the Holy Spirit sends a fresh anointing. He gives us renewed power to repel the attacks of the devil. He sends healing into the wounds of our lives. He restores our souls so we can move forward along paths of righteousness.

PREPARING FOR THIS FAST

Jesus taught very clearly that seeking God and His righteousness are to be at the top of our priority list. He said, "Seek ye first the kingdom of God, and his righteousness; and all these things shall be added unto you" (Matt. 6:33). What must we do to make God's righteousness our top priority? We should begin a season of prayer and fasting by seeking to answer this question.

As you prepare to establish a path of righteousness in life:

First, commit to a serious study of what it means to be righteous according to the Word of God. I encourage you to consult a concordance and make a list of all the references that are related to *righteousness* and *right standing*. As part of your prayer times, look up these references and write your insights about what the Lord is revealing to you.

Second, reevaluate your personal walk with the Lord. Are you where you truly desire to be in your relationship with the Lord? Are you growing toward spiritual maturity? Are you being conformed into the image of Christ Jesus? (See Rom. 8:29.)

Third, reevaluate your spiritual disciplines: the time you spend reading the Bible, the time you spend in prayer, the time you spend in church-related activities and worship, the time you spend with Christian friends, and the time you spend in ministry to others.

As you enter a season of praying and fasting for greater purity in your life, ask the Lord to establish you in a path of righteousness. The Lord's desire is for you to be steadfast in your Christian walk. Embrace the truth of God's Word about His desire as expressed in the book of 1 Peter: "The God of all grace . . . make you perfect, stablish, strengthen, settle you" (5:10).

Before the Lord can ever establish a people—a church, a body of believers, a family—in righteousness, He must establish individual people in righteousness. Make it your prayer: "Lord, start a revival, and begin the work in me."

Anticipating the Lies of the Devil

The devil seems to come with a vengeance after those who seek righteousness. The devil will do his utmost to get you off track and destroy any reputation for righteousness that you have before other people. He will tell you:

- "You can't live up to God's standards. Nobody can. You might as well not try."
- "The Bible gives an ideal—nobody ever actually lives that way."
- "You don't have what it takes to be a real Christian."
- "You have too many character flaws to ever become like Jesus."
- "You have sinned and as a result, God can never use you in ministry."

Lies, lies, and more lies! The devil is an accuser. His accusations, however, never stand up before God when they are about those who have made Jesus Christ their Savior and Lord! (See Rev. 12:10.) The Bible declares that Jesus is our righteousness. All the righteousness we ever have or hope to have is because of

Him. Jesus imparts His righteousness to us . . . and therefore, we stand in righteousness before God the Father because of who He is in us.

PRAYING FOR THE ESTABLISHMENT OF RIGHTEOUSNESS

As you pray during this fast, focus on what it means to be righteous and on how much importance God places on righteousness:

- If ye will obey my voice indeed, and keep my covenant, then ye shall be a peculiar treasure unto me above all people: for all the earth is mine: and ye shall be unto me a kingdom of priests, and an holy nation. (Exodus 19:5–6)
- For what is a man profited, if he shall gain the whole world, and lose his own soul? Or what shall a man give in exchange for his soul? (Matthew 16:26)
- Let thine eyes look right on, and let thine eyelids look straight before thee. Ponder the path of thy feet, and let all thy ways be established. Turn not to the right hand nor to the left: remove thy foot from evil. (Proverbs 4:25–27)

Praise and Thanksgiving for the Lord's Establishing You

As you pray and fast, be sure to recall and thank the Lord for the many ways in which He has preserved and established you. He has brought you this far! He will not abandon you now!

- "Thank You, Lord, for Your great mercy."
- "Thank You, Lord, for keeping me alive to this moment so I might confront areas of weakness in my life and walk in renewed righteousness before You."
- "Thank You, Lord, for revealing to me areas in which I need to remove obstacles to righteousness."

Praise the Lord for being the Author and Finisher of your faith (see Heb. 12:2).

Praise the Lord that He is the one who sees your beginning from your ending, and who will make a way for you to be established in righteousness.

Praying Specifically for God's Righteousness to Be Established

Ask the Lord to help you stay on His straight and narrow path.

Ask Him to show you areas of weakness in your life and ways in which you can strengthen these areas with His help.

Ask the Lord to purify and refine your life so you might better reflect Him to others.

18

THE REVEALING OF GOD'S GLORY

Very few of us can even begin to fathom the fullness of God's glory. The Old Testament speaks of times when God's *shekinah* filled the temple—people felt, saw, and experienced His presence in such fullness that no words could truly describe the wonder and majesty of the Lord. Don't we all long for that to be our experience? We want to catch a glimpse of His glory—and when we do, we can hardly contain the joy!

One of the key purposes for fasting, according to Isaiah 58, is that the "glory of the LORD shall be thy rearward" (v. 8).

A person once said to me, "I think there's a misspelled word in my Bible."

I said, "What's that?"

She pointed to this word "rearward" and said, "Shouldn't that be *reward*?"

Certainly the Lord is the giver of all rewards (see Heb. 11:6). But this word "rearward" has a very wonderful meaning in the language of the King James Version of the Bible. It refers to the glory of the Lord following behind you. His glory appears in the wake of your life. In many ways, the presence of the Lord that you leave behind you is your true legacy on earth.

The Israelites left Egypt's slavery and bondage only to have Pharaoh's armies pursue them a few days later. The Israelites found themselves with the Red Sea before them and Pharaoh's armies just minutes behind them. Moses gave this word to the people: "Fear ye not, stand still, and see the salvation of the LORD. . . . The LORD shall fight for you, and ye shall hold your peace" (Exod. 14:13–14).

The Bible tells us that during that night,

> the angel of God, which went before the camp of Israel, removed, and went behind them; and the pillar of the cloud went from before their face, and stood behind them: and it came between the camp of the Egyptians and the camp of Israel; and it was a cloud and darkness to them, but it gave light by night to these: so that the one came not near the other all the night. (Exodus 14:19–20)

Even as God sent His angels and the sign of His presence to seal off the "rearward" of His people—forbidding them to go back or to be conquered—God was working a miracle for their *forward* journey the next day. "The LORD caused the sea to go back by a strong east wind all that night, and made the sea dry land, and the waters were divided" (Exod. 14:21). This was the path through which the children of Israel crossed the Red Sea.

What is God's message to us in this? God does not want you to go backward. He always calls you to stand still—to stand strong, to refuse to be moved—in the face of your enemies. He calls you to move forward in the paths that He has prepared for you. He sends His glory to protect you and seal you off from your enemies, even as He prepares for your future. How wonderful our Lord is to us!

THE FAST JEHOSHAPHAT CALLED FOR ALL JUDAH

King Jehoshaphat of Israel had an experience during his reign that was similar to the one the children of Israel experienced. A message came to Jehoshaphat that he was about to be attacked by three mighty armies that had come together to defeat the Israelites. Soldiers of Moabites, Ammonites, and people from Mount Seir had gathered just miles from Jerusalem. The Bible tells us, "Jehoshaphat feared, and set himself to seek the LORD, and proclaimed a fast throughout all Judah." The people of Judah "gathered themselves together, to ask help of the LORD" and "to seek the LORD" (2 Chron. 20:3–4). Never had there been a time when these people were more desperate for God's help and guidance.

Feeling desperate is not necessarily a bad thing if it drives you to seek God in prayer and fasting. Feelings of desperation about a situation may very well be the way the Holy Spirit brings you to the place where He can show you His glory.

King Jehoshaphat led the way in prayer. He stood among the congregation and cried out to God. He began his prayer with praise, acknowledging that no power or might could withstand God. He then said humbly before the Lord, "We have no might against this great company that cometh against us; neither know we what to do: but our eyes are upon thee" (2 Chron. 20:12).

The Bible tells us that Judah stood before the Lord, with "their little ones, their wives, and their children" (2 Chron. 20:13). The people stood as one body before God. Entire families joined together in this time of praying and fasting.

Never exclude your family from a season of praying and fasting. Your spouse and children may not feel led to join you—invite them nevertheless. Give them an opportunity to come before God with you as you pray and fast for any of the purposes we have discussed in this book. God seeks to make your family a light to the world, to establish your family in righteousness, and to reveal His glory through your family.

A prophet of the Lord then stood in the midst of the congregation that had gathered together in Jerusalem and he gave the Lord's plan to the people: "Be not afraid nor dismayed by reason of this great multitude; for the battle is not yours, but God's" (2 Chron. 20:15). The prophet went on to give the location of the enemy and the way the enemy would attack. He said to the people, "Ye shall not need to fight in this battle: set yourselves, stand ye still, and see the salvation of the LORD with you" (2 Chron. 20:17).

I want you especially to note how Jehoshaphat and the people responded to this word from the Lord: "Jehoshaphat bowed his head with his face to the ground: and all Judah and the inhabitants of Jerusalem fell before the LORD, worshipping the LORD." Then the praise leaders of the people "stood up to praise the LORD God of Israel with a loud voice on high" (2 Chron. 20:18–19).

The next morning Jehoshaphat sent praise singers to go before the army, singing, "Praise the LORD; for his mercy endureth for ever." As the people went out to face their enemies with the choir leading the way, "the LORD sent ambushments" against the enemies and these three enemy armies fought until they completely destroyed one another (2 Chron. 20:21–22).

When the Israelites arrived on the scene, they saw only dead bodies and a tremendous amount of spoil and riches, including precious jewels. Rather than fight, the people of God spent three days gathering the spoil! On the fourth day they gathered again and "blessed the LORD" (2 Chron. 20:26). They returned to Jerusalem singing and praising God with great joy because the Lord had won the victory He had promised.

Not only did God's people know that the Lord had won the battle, all the nations around Israel knew it. A great fear of God came on these countries and "the realm of Jehoshaphat was quiet: for his God gave him rest round about" (2 Chron. 20:30).

In Retrospect

We can do nothing as human beings to make the glory of the Lord appear. The very nature of God's glory is rooted in the truth that God reveals Himself when He desires to do so—all things are according to His purposes and His timing. What we can do is see the glory of the Lord as we look rearward. We see how the Lord has worked in retrospect.

Before the battle we are always in a position of standing in faith. It is before the battle that our believing must be the strongest.

During the battle we see God's mighty hand at work on our behalf . . . or in some cases, we may not see God at work but rather see the effects of God's work. The people of Judah did not see their enemies kill one another; it was only after they had done so that the people of Judah came to a watchtower and looked out in the wilderness and saw the corpses of their enemies (2 Chron. 20:24).

It is after the battle—after the enemy is defeated, after the spoils have been gathered, after the peace begins to reign—that we see God's glory.

Look back over your life. See how God has worked. You'll have renewed faith to believe God to work in your current situation.

PREPARING FOR THIS FAST

In both the case of the Israelites at the Red Sea under the leadership of Moses, and in this case of the Israelites surrounded by enemies under the leadership of Jehoshaphat, the Lord revealed His glory both to encourage His people and to discourage—destroy and deter—their enemies.

This is what we seek as we enter a time of prayer and fasting for the glory of the Lord to be revealed. We are seeking God's encouragement and a mighty victory over someone or something that is attacking us. At the same time, we are seeking God to use this victory as a witness to our enemies that He is a great and awesome God who alone is worthy to be served.

As you prepare to pray and fast for God to win a victory on your behalf:

First, read through the experiences of Moses, the children of Israel, and the Jehoshaphat for yourself. Underline or highlight passages that the Lord reveals to you. Write down insights the Lord gives you as to how He desires for you to pray during your time of fasting.

Second, determine at the outset that praise will be at the center of your prayers as you fast.

Third, broaden your perspective—and your prayers—beyond your own personal need. Focus on needs that relate to your family, your church, your community, and your nation. The glory of the Lord was revealed to Moses and the whole body of the Israelites. The glory of the Lord was revealed to Jehoshaphat and all of Judah.

Anticipating the Lies of the Devil

As you pray and fast, the devil will come to you with lies about the way in which God works for your total deliverance—defeating your enemies behind you and preparing a way of escape before you. Get ready for his lies:

- "*You* have to do something."
- "You *have* to do something."
- "You have to *do* something."
- "You have to do *something*."
- "It's better to run and be safe than to just stand and wait."

- "It's better to compromise now and worry about other consequences later."
- "Time is running out. You need to act now."

Lies, lies, and more lies! Let the devil know that you are going to do things God's way and in God's timing—and that you aren't going to act until God shows you what to do and when to do it.

PRAYING THE TRUTH OF GOD AS YOU
ANTICIPATE GOD'S VICTORY

As you pray and fast, focus your Bible reading on miraculous instances in which God won a victory for His people without their having to fight a bloody battle. Three of the major examples of this are:

1. Gideon and a battle of the Israelites against the Midianites. (Judg. 7)
2. David and a battle against the Philistines. (1 Chron. 14:13–17)
3. The siege of the Syrians against Jerusalem. (2 Kings 7)

Also focus on verses in the Bible that remind you that we are called to give God the glory for all victories, wonders, and miracles that we experience:

- Thine is the kingdom, and the power, and the glory, for ever. (Matthew 6:13)
- The heavens declare the glory of God; and the firmament sheweth his handywork. (Psalm 19:1)
- Thou art worthy, O Lord, to receive glory and honour and power: for thou hast created all things, and for thy pleasure they are and were created. (Revelation 4:11)

- Fear God, and give glory to him; for the hour of his judgment is come: and worship him that made heaven, and earth, and the sea, and the fountains of waters. (Revelation 14:7)
- Give unto the LORD, O ye mighty, give unto the LORD glory and strength. Give unto the LORD the glory due unto his name; worship the LORD in the beauty of holiness. (Psalm 29:1–2)
- Not unto us, O LORD, not unto us, but unto thy name give glory, for thy mercy, and for thy truth's sake. (Psalm 115:1)

Praise and Thanksgiving for God's Victories

Focus your thanksgiving on the many ways in which God has brought you a victory in the past. It may have been a win over a real enemy who was persecuting you, a victory over a disease, a victory in a legal matter, or a victory over a financial matter. Thank the Lord for very specific instances in which God made a way where there seemed to be no way.

- "Thank You, Heavenly Father, for the way in which You have defeated my enemies."
- "Thank You, Heavenly Father, for paving a way of success and revival in my future."
- "Thank You, Heavenly Father, for helping me trust You in difficult times."

Praise the Lord that Jesus is the Victor over all things that seek to harm us.

Praise Jesus that He is the Giver of an abundant life—that He is the one who reverses all things that the devil does to steal, kill, and destroy us (see John 10:10).

Praise the Lord that He is capable of defeating any and every foe (see Isa. 59:1).

Praying Specifically for Victory That Reveals God's Glory

Ask the Lord to show you His plan for the way to address an enemy or an evil situation that is coming against your life, your family, your church, your neighborhood, your city, or your nation.

Pray that others around you will feel convicted of their sins and desire to establish righteousness so that you and your family might dwell in a peaceful environment.

Pray that your leaders might have God's wisdom as they lead you to battle the enemy of your souls.

19

A TURNING POINT FOR GOD'S "NEW THING"

Some of the most spectacular examples of fasting in the Bible are the forty-day fasts of the great lawgiver Moses (and Joshua his assistant), the prophet Elijah, and Jesus. Each of these fasts established something new that God desired on the earth. God called each of these men specifically to undertake this length of fasting, and the Spirit prepared each specifically before he undertook his fast.

A person should never conclude, *Well, Moses fasted forty days so I should too.* No! A fast of that length could be very dangerous for you. If the Lord leads you to undertake a fast of this length, He will call you, and then He will prepare you for it in very specific ways. Forty days is a long time—and a fast of that length might kill a person or cause serious health problems if he does it without the Spirit's leading. I truly believe that Moses, Elijah, and Jesus could endure forty days of fasting only because the Spirit led them to do this . . . and the Spirit enabled them each day.

KEY PRINCIPLES OF THE FORTY-DAY FASTS

There are several key principles in these fasts, however, that we can and should apply to our own seasons of praying and fasting.

The Call of God to Confront Evil

What purpose did God have for those He called to prolonged periods of fasting? I believe it was a call to confront evil—both evil circumstances and manifestations that are outside a person, as well as the evil influences of fear and discouragement that form inside a person. Some people face unrelenting and devastating evil circumstances or people.

God called Moses, Elijah, and Jesus to showdown moments against the devil.

The Call of God to Personal Victory

God called Moses to encourage, renew, and prepare him to lead the Israelites in obeying the commandments of God. Moses' time of fasting came after Moses had erupted in anger and destroyed the first set of tablets God had given him. It came at a time of great personal discouragement and a feeling of defeat in Moses' life. The fast ended with Moses receiving a second set of tablets, and the power of the Holy Spirit poured out on him in such a powerful way that when Moses returned to the people, the people not only desired to keep the Law but were eager to keep it.

God called Elijah to encourage, renew, and prepare him to move forward in leading the Israelites against their spiritual enemies. His time of fasting came after Elijah had destroyed the prophets of Baal and a wicked queen had then threatened him. The fast came at a time of great personal discouragement and a feeling of defeat in Elijah's life. The fast ended with Elijah receiving directives and a renewed anointing of the Holy Spirit so he might set up new political and spiritual leadership among the Israelites for the coming decades.

God called Jesus to enter a time of fasting so Jesus might have a definitive victory over His own humanity and pave the way for God's new covenant with mankind.

The Call of God That Brings Profound Change

Those God called to these forty-day fasts were leaders. In fact, each was the leader of his day. Moses was the leader of the Israelites. Elijah was the prophet of the Lord to the children of Israel. Jesus was the Son of God sent to redeem mankind.

Things were not the same in these leaders' lives after their times of fasting. In fact, life was very different. For Moses, life after his fast meant the Law of God framed his life. For Elijah, life after his fast meant a new order of leadership in the land—two new kings and a new prophet. For Jesus, life after His fast meant an intense three years of ministry—preaching, teaching, and healing—that would culminate in His death on the cross and resurrection from the tomb.

Things were not the same in the lives of the people who were under the leadership of these three men after their time of fasting. Time and eternity were altered. For the Israelites, the fast of Moses meant the giving of the Law to them. They lived under a new order of feasts, rituals, sacrifices, and patterns of worship. For the Israelites in the time of Elijah, the fast of Elijah resulted in their having a new wave of righteousness in their land—including powerful miracles at the hand of Elisha, the successor of Elijah. For the Jews in the time of Jesus and for all of us who have lived since that time, the fast of Jesus resulted in Jesus stripping the devil of all claims he had made. Jesus assumed full authority over nature, over the systems of mankind, and over the heavenly realm—remaining fully subject to God the Father, but never subject to the devil or evil people under the devil's influence. Jesus laid claim to the authority to act upon God's Word in ways that brought healing and deliverance to people, and because He did, fully sealing that authority on the cross, Jesus was able to pass on to us the authority to act upon God's Word in ways that bring healing and deliverance to those in need.

The call of God to a prolonged fast is not for everybody. It is for those whom God chooses and whom God calls for very specific purposes. (Before commencing a fast, you should assess your health and consider visiting a health professional.)

God Gives the Strength for a Fast

God gave each of these leaders the strength for his fast. When God calls a person to undertake a fast of any length—or to undertake any task—God gives the person strength to persevere and succeed. We see this very clearly in Elijah's fast.

Elijah was defeated in his spirit at the time God called and prepared him for a prolonged fast. He had built an altar to the Lord in a showdown match with 450 prophets of a false god named Baal. Then Elijah had called down fire at Mount Carmel—a supernatural sign of God's acceptance of Elijah's sacrifice. This was a tremendous victory for the Lord as the Lord displayed His awesome power! When the people saw the fire of the Lord, and how it consumed the burnt sacrifice that Elijah prepared—as well as the wood and stones and dust of the altar Elijah had built, and as well as the water in the trench Elijah had dug around the altar—the people fell on their faces before God. They cried out, "The LORD, he is the God; the LORD, he is the God" (1 Kings 18:39). Elijah then ordered that the prophets of Baal be killed by the brook at the base of the mountain.

In the aftermath of this, Elijah had prayed for rain to fall on the drought-stricken land, and God opened the heavens in response to his prayer. Then, with the sky turning black with clouds, wind, and torrential rain, Elijah ran before Ahab's chariot into Jezreel.

Elijah had experienced a supernatural anointing of strength

for that day—a day unlike any in history before or since. You'd think he would have been on top of the world.

So why was Elijah feeling defeated? When he returned to Jezreel, Elijah received a message from Queen Jezebel. She was furious at what had happened on Mount Carmel—the deaths of the 450 prophets to Baal that she had personally supported and sponsored. She sent a death threat to Elijah, saying, "So let the gods do to me, and more also, if I make not thy life as the life of one of them by to morrow about this time" (1 Kings 19:2).

Elijah ran for his life in a weak moment of fear. He allowed the great faith that had prompted the revival of the nation to evaporate from his own heart. He had courageously and boldly entered a showdown with 450 men, but he could not stand up to one woman. Elijah ran from the city toward the south.

He eventually made his way to Beersheba, which was about a hundred miles south of Jezreel. Elijah was far from home and far from Jezebel at that point, yet he still didn't feel he had escaped. He went another day's journey into the wilderness— probably twenty to thirty miles into the desert. And there, he sat down under a juniper tree and asked God to end his life. He said, "It is enough; now, O LORD, take away my life; for I am not better than my fathers" (1 Kings 19:4).

Elijah slept under that juniper tree, and the Bible tells us that an angel touched him and said, "Arise and eat." Elijah saw a cake baking on the coals of a fire and a jug of water at his head. He rose and ate the cake and drank the water, then lay down again. The angel of the Lord came a second time, touched him, and said, "Arise and eat; because the journey is too great for thee." Elijah rose and ate and drank a second time and then we read that he "went in the strength of that meat forty days and forty nights unto Horeb the mount of God" (1 Kings 19:5, 7–8).

God prepared Elijah with both physical rest for his body and sufficient food for his body before his long trek to Horeb, which was another 180 miles to the south. His journey from the juniper tree to Horeb took significantly longer than his trip from Jezreel to Beersheba. The trip to the juniper tree probably took Elijah about a week. The trip to Horeb took almost six weeks!

What really happened when the angel of the Lord touched Elijah and gave him food and water? Those elements were more than physical provision. They strengthened and encouraged Elijah in his spirit for the long trek to the mountain of the Lord, the same mountain where Moses had received the Ten Commandments.

Elijah had fled to the south, seemingly as far away from Jezebel as he could go. God called him to go even farther south so that He might speak to him. Lying under the juniper tree, Elijah had been so depressed that he wanted to die. When the angel touched him and made provision for him, Elijah had a renewed sense of purpose and a renewed desire to hear from God.

Under the juniper tree, Elijah was doing the talking. On Mount Horeb, Elijah was doing the listening. The time of fasting between the juniper tree and Horeb was God's time of preparing Elijah to hear from Him in order that Elijah might experience a threefold renewal: a renewal of his faith, a renewal of his reliance upon the Word of the Lord, and a renewal of his hope for the future.

Elijah found himself eventually in a cave on Mount Horeb. Again, this is very much like the experience of Moses, so let's recall Moses' experience.

God Reverses a Negative Situation

God used these fasts to reverse very negative situations. He began that reversal in the heart and mind of the leader himself. In our lives, God speaks first to us before He speaks to others under our leadership. He speaks first to us about the state of our own hearts and souls.

Let me recall some of the details of Moses' experience.

God had called Moses to come up on Mount Horeb, also called Mount Sinai, and there, God had given him the Law of

His covenant with Israel, which Moses wrote on tablets of stone. Moses had also been in a cave of some type, for when the Lord told Moses that He would reveal His goodness to him, He said to Moses, "I will put thee in a clift of the rock, and will cover thee with my hand while I pass by" so that Moses would not see the Lord's face (Exod. 33:22).

Moses was "there with the LORD forty days and forty nights; he did neither eat bread, nor drink water" (Exod. 34:28).

This was not the first time that Moses had gone up the mountain to meet with God. The first time, the Lord had given him commandments, and Moses had returned with the Law of God to the camp of the Israelites at the base of the mountain. There he found the Israelites feasting before and dancing around the image of a golden calf that they made as an idol.

Moses had become so angry at the people's actions that he broke the tablets on which the Law was written. He confronted those who worshiped before the golden calf and he called the sons of Levi—the priests—to slay all who had worshiped the false god. They killed nearly three thousand Israelites. Then Moses called the priests to repent of their sin in allowing this false idol to be made, even as Moses called upon God to forgive their sin. The Lord then said to Moses, "Depart, and go up hence" (Exod. 33:1).

Do you see the similarities in the experiences of Elijah and Moses? Both men were anointed for a very special task of faith—they saw tremendous manifestations of God's power— and then the evil actions of others seemed to drain away their faith.

Moses spoke words to God that were very similar to Elijah's, in essence saying to the Lord, if You won't forgive the people, "blot me, I pray thee, out of thy book which thou hast written" (Exod. 32:32).

Moses and Elijah had this in common: both men thought they were at the end of what God had called them to do. They could not fathom that God might have something more, even greater, for them to do. They thought their ministries—their reasons for being—were over. They saw themselves as used up, finished. They were depleted of vision and hope.

What happened to Moses during his forty days and forty nights on Mount Horeb? God renewed his faith, his vision, his ministry. Moses again wrote the commandments and words of the covenant on tables of stone. And when Moses came down from the mountain this second time, the Bible tells us that "the skin of his face shone" so brightly that the people insisted he cover his face with a veil (Exod. 34:30). Moses had not only heard from God, he had experienced God's glory.

And Elijah? When Elijah found himself in a cave on Mount Horeb, the word of the Lord came to him and asked, "What doest thou here, Elijah?" Elijah replied, "I have been very jealous for the LORD God of hosts: for the children of Israel have forsaken thy covenant, thrown down thine altars, and slain thy prophets with the sword; and I, even I only, am left; and they seek my life, to take it away" (1 Kings 19:9–10).

The Lord told Elijah to go stand at the entrance to the cave and the Lord caused a tremendous wind to pass by, then an earthquake, then a fire. And Elijah knew God was not in the wind or the earthquake or the fire.

Elijah had been looking at manifestations of God's power, rather than focusing on God as the source of all power. There's a difference. We can become highly discouraged when we look for God in manifestations and don't see Him. We begin to think that God is no longer with us. It is in this fasting time that Elijah recognized that while God manifests His power in whatever way He chooses—allowing and even sending manifestations of His power into our midst—not all manifestations on earth convey a message from God.

Then God sent a "still small" voice and when Elijah heard it, "he wrapped his face in his mantle, and went out, and stood in the entering in of the cave. And, behold, there came a voice unto him, and said, What doest thou here, Elijah?" (1 Kings 19:12–13).

Elijah had heard the voice of an angry queen resonating in his mind. He had heard the voice of evil threatening him and discouraging him. Now, in this moment on the mountain of God, Elijah began to hear the voice of the living God—a still, small voice. Elijah had no doubt that it was God. That was the reason he covered his face: just as in the case of Moses, Elijah knew that God would not reveal His glory to him face-to-face.

God Brings Us to a Place of Total Submission

God asked Elijah the same question—He spoke to him a second time just as the Lord had spoken His covenant and commandments to Moses a second time. And this time, Elijah was prepared in his heart to listen and to obey regardless of what any other person did. Fear was not going to thwart his obedience. The response of others was not going to influence him. Like Moses, Elijah had reached a place of total submission and reliance upon the Lord without any concern for others' behavior or evil intent.

God Gives Us Instructions for Our Good and the Good of Others

Elijah, no doubt, had a clear revelation of how he had missed God and failed to rely upon the leading of the Spirit in all things. Elijah listened closely to the Lord's still, small voice and God gave him very specific instructions. God told him where to go: to Damascus, three hundred miles to the north, even farther north than his starting place, which meant Elijah had to go through the territory where Jezebel still ruled. The Lord told Elijah specifically what he was to do: anoint Hazael to be king over Syria, anoint Jehu to be king over Israel, and anoint Elisha to be prophet after Elijah. And finally, the Lord encouraged Elijah by revealing to him that there were still seven thousand people in Israel who had not bowed in worship to Baal.

Both of these fasts—the fast of Elijah and the fast of Moses—are related in many ways to the fast that the Holy Spirit led Jesus to make in the wilderness.

THE FAST OF JESUS

Just as Elijah and Moses did not seek to fast before God called them, neither did Jesus. The Spirit led Him into the wilderness (Matt. 4:1).

God called Jesus, as He did Elijah and Moses, to pray and fast in order to institute God's new thing on the earth. In Moses' day, God wrote with His finger of fire on stone tablets. In Elijah's day, God instituted a new plan for spiritual leadership at a time when there was no righteousness in the land. In the example of Jesus, God was preparing to write a new law of love on human hearts.

Both Moses and Elijah were confronting major pagan forces in their day. Jesus, the Son of God, confronted the evil force behind all other pagan forces!

Each of these men embodied a different aspect of the word of the Lord. Moses received a written word. Elijah heard the spoken word of God. Jesus was the Word of God incarnate (John 1:1).

Each of these men faced an enemy. Moses faced the pagan beliefs that were still among the Israelites and his own anger. Elijah faced a wicked queen and his own discouragement. Jesus faced the devil and His own humanity that was subject to temptation.

Each man was successful in his fast, and successful in the work that God called him to do.

If God calls you to a prolonged fast, you can trust the Lord to help you every step of the way.

Some people question whether a person truly can complete a fast the length of those recorded for Moses, Elijah, and Jesus. The answer is a strong yes. (Before commencing a fast, you should assess your health and consider visiting a health professional.)

Let me share with you the story of a medical doctor named Henry S. Tanner, who lived in the 1880s. Dr. Tanner sought to prove that fasting could improve a person's health. At that time, physicians and theologians both ridiculed him, not believing that a person could survive a prolonged fast.

At the age of fifty, under strict supervision, Dr. Tanner fasted for forty-three days. The newspapers covered the story. At the conclusion of the fast he claimed to have had a vision of heaven, angels, and the Lord Jesus Christ. He became a pioneer for the advancement of fasting and routinely taught and prescribed fasting to his patients.

At the age of sixty, Dr. Tanner fasted for fifty days. In the middle of this fast he had a vision of "the unspeakable glories of God." He came out of that fast feeling thirty years younger. People remarked that he appeared to be forty years old instead of sixty.

At the age of seventy-seven, Dr. Tanner fasted for fifty-three days. As an outcome of that fast, his gray hair was replaced by new black hair! It was the same color as it was when he was a young man.

Dr. Tanner died at the age of ninety-three.

Always be aware that fasting is not a competition—not with other people who are fasting or with yourself. There's no benefit in seeing how much you can fast or in trying to set a personal fasting record.

Fasting does not bring an automatic reward of righteousness. In other words, a person who fasts is not automatically more righteous than a person who does not fast. The Lord hands out no blue ribbons for fasters. The real benefit to fasting comes when fasting is linked to prayer. It is the focus on prayer that releases the righteousness of the Lord into our lives.

GOD'S NEW THING THROUGH YOU

God often brings us to a season of praying and fasting so He might do a new thing in us . . . and also through us. In most cases, He will not call us to such a prolonged fast. His desire, nonetheless, may be to do a new thing.

Ask God in your time of praying and fasting if there is something that He desires you to establish. Through the centuries, many have established ministries as the result of praying and fasting.

As you pray and fast, read the Bible with new intensity. Open your heart to hearing the written Word of God. Stay close to Christian leaders who operate in the fullness of God's Spirit. Open your heart to hearing the *rhema* or spoken word of the Lord from God's prophets today. Stay in prayer. Listen closely for the Holy Spirit to speak deep within your heart.

Consider the possibility of going into a season of fasting and praying simply and solely to hear from God. Use this time to see if God has something to say to you. Go into a time of praying and fasting with a clean slate and no agenda.

Recognize that if God truly is calling you to establish a new ministry or work for Him, you are going to face intense opposition. First and foremost, that opposition will be spiritual. You will need to engage in spiritual warfare as never before. Moses, Elijah, and Jesus each faced the most intense forms of spiritual warfare.

Recognize that you will face your own weaknesses and frailties as never before. You will be forced to confront your own humanity—perhaps your own anger or discouragement, as did Moses and Elijah. You will be tempted, perhaps most of all, not to obey the call of God into a new area of ministry.

Recognize that you likely will face some human opposition as well. People will discourage you, question you, and perhaps even ridicule you.

Go into your fast with a commitment to:

- *Obey.* Make it your heart's desire to obey God.
- *Persevere.* Anticipate that you will face obstacles if God calls you to a new thing. Set your heart to persevere until you've accomplished God's goal.
- *Receive.* Expect to come out of your fast with a clear blessing and a clear direction from the Lord.

I have absolutely no doubt that if we will do our part in obeying and persevering, God will act on our behalf and He will use us to accomplish His purposes. God desires to pour out His delivering and healing power on you. God desires to use you in ever-increasing ways to bring glory to His name and to extend His kingdom.

Furthermore, the more you pray and fast, the more benefit you will find in fasting and praying. The Lord will teach you more about praying and fasting as you pray and fast.

Trust God to work in you mightily as you seek His face! In my life there is no substitute for praying and fasting. I firmly believe you will come to that same conclusion the more you pray and fast.

APPENDIX

DAILY JOURNAL FOR A TWENTY-ONE-DAY SEASON OF FASTING AND PRAYING

DAY of the Fast:

DATE:

Theme or Focus of the Day:

Bible Verse for the Day:

Specific Prayer for the Day:

Insights, Special Experiences, Ideas, or Other Notes about the Day: